A BRIEF HISTORY OF ANCIENT GREECE

TRAVELING THE HELLENISTIC WORLD: AN ODYSSEY THROUGH POLITICAL DYNASTIES AND CULTURAL MOSAICS

DOMINIC HAYNES

Ebook ISBN: 978-1-915710-47-5
Paperback ISBN: 978-1-915710-48-2
Hardcover ISBN: 978-1-915710-49-9
Published by: Dominic Haynes History

CONTENTS

MESSAGE TO THE READER

As you embark on this enlightening journey through the annals of Ancient Greece, we wanted to offer a few tools to enhance your experience further.

Companion PDF: We understand that the vivid tales of history can sometimes come alive even more with a visual touch. To this end, we've prepared a companion PDF. This guide contains images shedding light on the key architecture and iconic artifacts we'll explore in the pages ahead. All items with a superscript number within this book will have a corresponding image in the PDF. To access this PDF, scan the QR code below.

A Surprise Ebook, Just for You: Your passion for history is something we deeply cherish. As a small token of our appreciation, we've curated a special on-hour long surprise history ebook. To lay claim to this gift, all you need to do is join our email community and we'll send it directly to your inbox. Once in the community, you will also get free access to all our future books and have your say in what we write about next. To join, scan the QR code below or click on the image (if you're reading this on ebook).

We are genuinely excited and honored to guide you through the captivating epochs of Ancient Greece. Trust that these additional resources will add depth and dimension to your expedition.

Warmly,
Dominic Haynes History

Companion PDF

Surprise Ebook

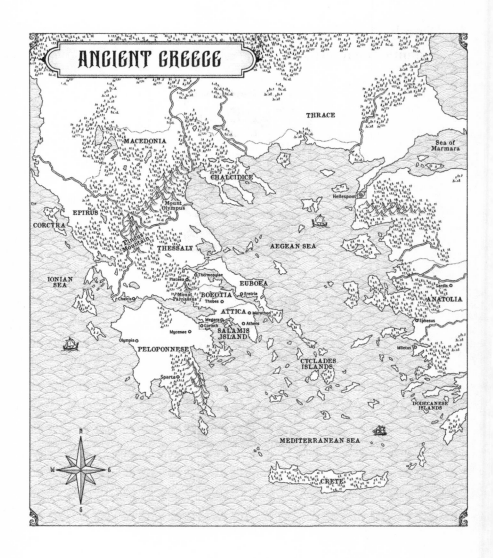

INTRODUCTION

Toward the eastern edge of the Mediterranean Sea lies a vibrant, forested peninsula adorned with rugged mountains. A spray of islands radiate from the mainland and nestle in the famously azure waters of the Aegean Sea. It is here, among the tangles of the olive trees, that the story of Ancient Greece unfolds. Here, the interwoven threads of myth and reality, intellect and valor, join with an unwavering quest for human excellence, building a narrative that traverses the ages.

This journey through the annals of Ancient Greece will navigate the intricacies and contradictions of this remarkable civilization. Witness the ascent of the city-states, each serving as a unique experiment of culture and politics, from Athens, the cradle of democracy, to Sparta, the bastion of martial discipline. Stand on the battlefields of the Persian Wars, where a shared cause finally united the fractious Greek city-states. From there, bask in the brilliance of Athens' Golden Age, a time when the arts, philosophy, and politics converged to create a cultural zenith that still captivates the world.

Follow the corridors of Greek thought to the inception of philosophy, where luminaries like Socrates, Plato, and Aristotle contemplated the mysteries of existence, ethics, and the natural world. Marvel at the exquisite beauty of Greek art, from the enduring grace of their statues to the timeless narratives of their theater. Though Ancient Greece's time as the preeminent Mediterranean power did not last, their assimilation into the Roman Empire did not herald their erasure.

Even in the twilight of their sovereignty, the Greeks continued to cast a profound shadow, with their cultural and intellectual legacy permeating the world. As the Roman poet Horace remarked, "Captive Greece held captive her uncouth conqueror and brought the arts to the rustic Latin lands."

1

DAWN TO DUSK: FROM PREHISTORIC GREECE TO THE GREEK DARK AGES (10,000–C. 800 BCE)

Human habitation on the Greek islands and peninsula dates back to the Paleolithic Age (c. 3.3 million–130,000 BCE). In fact, within the Apidima Cave on the tip of the Peloponnesian Peninsula, the oldest set of human remains outside of Africa were discovered. Dated over 210,000 years ago, the discovery meant that *Homo sapiens* arrived in the Mediterranean region far earlier than once thought, forcing archaeologists and historians to reconsider the previously accepted dates for humanity's migration outside of the African continent.

Before continuing, it is helpful to ground the text in some geographical landmarks. The shape of the Grecian landscape has profoundly impacted the region's history and culture over the years. The Attic peninsula begins in the eastern portion of the mainland, later home to the area's well-known city of Athens. Attica boasts a rocky terrain that spills down to the Aegean Sea, making it a strategic hub for trade. To the southwest lies the Peloponnesian Peninsula, a landmass connected to the mainland by the narrow Isthmus of Corinth. Here, the famous Spartans and Corinthians eventually made their home. Another peninsula worth mentioning is the trident-shaped Chalcidice, a set of three peninsulas known today as the Halkidiki. This region resides in northeastern Greece, jutting into the Aegean Sea.

The Greek mainland itself is a patchwork of mountains, valleys, and plains, with the towering Pindus Mountains in the north contrasting with the fertile plains of Thessaly. The Aegean archipelago is scattered with picturesque islands, from Crete in the south to the Cyclades and the Dodecanese in the central and eastern regions.

Furthermore, the geographical reach of Ancient Greece extended beyond what is traditionally recognized as the nation of Greece in the present day. Two regions to be aware of are the Turkish coastline and the Hellespont. The Turkish coast, also called the Anatolian coast, stretches along the southwestern edge of the present-day nation of Türkiye, bordering the Aegean Sea to the west and the Mediterranean Sea to the south. The region now known as Asia Minor, most of which comprises the country of Türkiye, was known at the time as Anatolia. This region boasts a stunning and diverse landscape characterized by rugged mountains, idyllic bays, and fertile plains. Its remarkable beauty is matched only by its historical significance. The ancient city of Troy, situated in the region of Troas and renowned for the Trojan War described in Homer's epic, *Iliad*, once stood along this coast. Additionally, many other important ancient Greek cities were located on or near this coastline, like the city of Miletus.

The Hellespont, on the other hand, is a narrow strait that connects the Aegean Sea to the Sea of Marmara. It is known more commonly today as the Dardanelles or the Strait of Gallipoli. Ultimately, the Sea of Marmara narrows into the Bosporus Strait before emptying into the Black Sea. The city of Istanbul, known at various points in history as Byzantium or Constantinople, sits aside this strait.

This waterway has always been strategically important as a critical maritime passage connecting the Mediterranean to the Black Sea region. In antiquity, it was a key trade, exploration, and conquest route. It's most famously associated with the story of the Greek hero Leander, who swam the Hellespont each night to visit his lover, Hero. It is also where the Persian King Xerxes famously constructed a bridge of boats during his invasion of Greece, but more on that later.

By the Neolithic Age (10,000–2200 BCE) and the overlapping Bronze Age (3300–1200 BCE), permanent and sophisticated tribal presences existed throughout the Greek mainland and isles. The most memorable are the

Cycladic and Minoan cultures on the islands and the Mycenaean civilization on the mainland. Each is characterized by its unique traits and contributions.

The Cycladic culture, named for its location on the Cyclades in the Aegean archipelago, dates back to around 3200 BCE and is best known for its distinctive abstract art. Notably, Cycladic artisans crafted iconic marble figurines, portraying serene female forms with folded arms, exemplifying their artistic finesse. Although historical records are scarce, their maritime expertise and trading networks likely played a pivotal role in the interconnected Aegean during the Bronze Age.

Beyond maritime endeavors, the Cycladic culture thrived in agricultural pursuits, cultivating barley, wheat, and legumes and engaging in livestock farming. Their agricultural foundation supported an economically robust, artistically inclined, and highly self-sufficient society. Nonetheless, the Cycladic culture presents historical challenges due to the absence of a known written language, necessitating reliance on archaeological findings and comparative studies to unravel the enigmas of their society, beliefs, and history. During the later part of the Bronze Age, artifacts from the Minoan and Mycenaean cultures were discovered in the Cyclades. However, whether these artifacts indicate trade and interaction between the cultures or suggest political or military dominance over the region is uncertain.

Southwards, the island of Crete bore the Minoan civilization, a flourishing society inhabiting the region from around 3000 to 1400 BCE. The culture, though clearly existing in the archaeological and historical record, is also tangled in myth. Even the contemporary name of the culture comes from the legendary king of Crete, Minos. This figure, along with the story of Theseus, the Minotaur, and the labyrinth, heavily influences what is remembered of Minoan culture today.

It remains uncertain whether Minos and his legendary counterparts truly existed. However, archaeology can unveil some facts about the ancient people of Crete. They constructed grand palatial centers, with the Palace of Knossos as the most renowned example. These palaces were architectural marvels and multifunctional hubs, combining administrative, religious, and communal spaces. Their distinctive architecture featured multi-story buildings, frescoed walls, and advanced plumbing systems, showcasing the Minoans' engineering prowess.

Maritime supremacy was a defining feature of the Minoan civilization. Situated at the crossroads of Mediterranean trade routes, their island location favored naval activities. The Minoans were accomplished sailors and traders, establishing extensive networks for exchanging goods. This facilitated trade in commodities like pottery, metals, and textiles with neighboring civilizations, including Egypt and Anatolia.

Minoan art was characterized by its vivid and intricate frescoes, often depicting scenes of nature, rituals, and daily life. Their pottery displayed distinctive shapes and decorative patterns, marked by a vibrant color palette of red, blue, and green shades. The Minoans left behind a script known as Linear A, which remains undeciphered. This linguistic mystery adds to the complexity of understanding their written records fully.

The Minoan civilization, however, met an uncertain fate. Natural disasters, including earthquakes and volcanic eruptions, took their toll. Simultaneously, the Mycenaeans, a mainland Greek civilization, infiltrated the Minoan domain. Around 1400 BCE, the Palace of Knossos collapsed, signaling the decline of Minoan civilization and the onset of its integration into Mycenaean culture.

These Mycenaeans flourished during the Late Bronze Age, from approximately 1700 to 1100 BCE. Though these are not yet considered the "Ancient Greeks," the Mycenaeans were instrumental in shaping the foundation of what would become the more commonly recognized Ancient Greece of Athens and Sparta, Plato, and Socrates. Named after the city of Mycenae, one of its most renowned centers, the Mycenaean culture is characterized by several key features.

The Mycenaeans were exceptional builders, and their cities were known for their impressive fortifications, which included massive stone walls and fortresses. Prominent centers like Mycenae, Tiryns, and Pylos stood as bastions of Mycenaean power, showcasing these formidable defenses. Within the fortresses, palaces served as the nerve centers of their society, with multi-purpose complexes that played critical roles in administration, religious practices, and communal life. These palaces' imposing architectural designs and grandeur exemplify their importance in Mycenaean governance.

Crucially, the Mycenaeans developed the Linear B script, a writing system deciphered and recognized as an early form of the Greek language. Linear B, thought to be an adaptation of the Minoans' Linear A, was primarily used for record-keeping, particularly in the organization of inventories and administration.

Mycenaean society was steeped in martial traditions and often focused on the lives and narratives of its warriors. This is reflected in their epic tales, later immortalized in Homer's *Iliad* and *Odyssey*, filled with stories of heroic deeds, battles, and conquests. Here, you find the characters of Achilles, Agamemnon, Odysseus, Penelope, Helen of Troy, and more. These stories are well-recognized throughout present-day Western civilization and continue to spark excitement and curiosity, spawning countless literary and film adaptations.

As an aside, the Trojan War, though lauded as fact by the ancient Greeks, is up for scholarly debate. There is no consensus on whether the conflict occurred, nor are there clear dates within the historical record. The city of Troy was real, and archaeologists believe there is some evidence that armed clashes took place there, but there is no decisive proof of the veracity of the Trojan War.

The Mycenaeans were also active in trade and interacted with other civilizations, chiefly their Aegean contemporaries. Religion was significant in Mycenaean life, with various deities venerated through offerings and rituals conducted in palaces and regional sanctuaries. Their artistic expressions featured intricate designs and motifs, as seen in pottery, jewelry, and other artifacts. The Mycenaeans practiced polytheism, and many of their deities were integrated into the beliefs of their Greek successors.

The reasons for the Mycenaean civilization's decline continue to be a subject of discussion among historians. However, a combination of factors, including natural disasters, external invasions, and internal conflicts, are often cited as contributing to their ultimate collapse. One likely culprit was the arrival of the Dorian people from the northern portion of mainland Greece. This tribe swept down the Peloponnesian peninsula and largely displaced the Mycenaean population over time. Nevertheless, whether their decline was natural or caused by human action, it marked the conclusion of the Late Bronze Age and the transition to the subsequent eras of Greek history.

Before delving into the Dorians, it is necessary to take a brief detour into some of the tribal intricacies of mainland Greece. Like any other region, the ethnic makeup of Greece is multifaceted and stems from many sources. However, there is some ethnic commonality between the various Greek tribes.

To begin with, in their native language, modern Greeks refer to their country as "Ελλάδα" (Elláda) and call themselves "Έλληνες" (Éllines). The term "Hellas," an ancient name, is used in English to denote the same. The name traces back to Greek mythology, where Hellen is considered the progenitor of the main Greek tribes and, subsequently, all Greeks. From Hellen's name we derive terms such as "Hellenistic," which refers to the period and culture following Alexander the Great's conquests when Greek culture proliferated worldwide. It's important to note that Hellen is entirely distinct from Helen of Troy. They are separate figures, with Hellen being a foundational figure for the Greeks, while Helen is famously tied to the events of the Trojan War.

As the story goes, Hellen was the king of Phthia, a region in Thessaly on the eastern coast of Greece and the ancestral home of Achilles' legendary Myrmidons. He was the son of Deucalion (the Greek equivalent of Noah) and Pyrrha, and the grandson of the Titan Prometheus. Hellen had three sons, Aeolus, Dorus, and Xuthus. Xuthus went on to have two sons of his own, Ion and Achaeus. It is from the names of Hellen's sons and grandsons that the four tribal names of the Greeks can be derived: Aeolians, Achaeans, Dorians, and Ionians.

These groups have slight religious and linguistic differences but are all recognized as ethnically Greek. The Aeolians chiefly resided around the region of Thessaly but later spread to other portions of Greece and Asia Minor. The Achaeans have already been discussed since they are typically recognized by another name: the Mycenaeans. As mentioned earlier, they first lived in the Peloponnesian peninsula, and a contingent of them are thought to have fled to Cyprus during the Dorian invasion. As for the Ionians, they mostly lived in the eastern portion of Greece, particularly on the Attic peninsula and many of the Aegean islands. During the Dorian invasion, a cohort of Ionians—like the Aeolians and Achaeans—left the Greek mainland and settled on the western coast of Anatolia.

As for the Dorians, they were likely natives of the regions of northwestern Greece and Macedonia. At some point, traditionally dated around the 12th century BCE, the Dorians began to migrate into Greece's southern and central regions. This movement is believed to have been accompanied by military conquest and the establishment of new Doric city-states. The implications of this event were profound and far-reaching, marking a significant transition from the Late Bronze Age to the early Iron Age, a period often referred to as the Greek Dark Ages.

The exact causes of the Dorian invasion remain a subject of historical debate. Some scholars posit factors such as population pressures, political turmoil, or external threats as potential drivers. Others argue it may have been a gradual migration rather than a full-scale invasion. The Greek historian Thucydides, who lived during the 5th century BCE, characterizes the arrival of the Dorians as a series of migrations that "re-settled" Greece.

Regardless of the exact nature of this movement, its impact on Greek history is undeniable. The Dorians settled in various regions, including the Peloponnese, establishing prominent city-states such as Sparta. The ensuing political, social, and cultural changes laid the groundwork for the next phase of Greek civilization.

This was a period of upheaval in the Greek mainland and islands. With the powerful Mycenaeans weakened and unseated, the bellicose Dorians sweeping over the mainland, and companies of Aeolians and Ionians fleeing eastward to Anatolia, much of the social structure and order broke down. The result, as mentioned earlier, was the Greek Dark Ages. Similar to Europe's Dark Ages, it's not that this period was devoid of significant events; it was a time of considerable upheaval and activity. The term "Dark Ages" primarily indicates a gap or scarcity in the historical record. Like the fall of Rome, the fall of Mycenae was undoubtedly disruptive and devastating to the denizens of Greece.

In history, events are named by those who live beyond them, not by those actively living in them. As such, they can be misunderstood, mischaracterized, or overly simplified. Renaissance thinkers labeled the preceding years as a "Dark Age," much like Classical Greek scholars viewed the eras of their forebears. Yet more occurred during the Greek Dark Ages than typically thought. It was during the later stages of this era, around the 8th century BCE, that Homer's epic poems, the *Iliad* and the *Odyssey*, were likely composed and orally transmitted. While these poems are set in an earlier time, their formation and dissemination are closely linked to the Greek Dark Ages. These timeless works preserved the memory of the Mycenaean world and embodied the evolving values and narratives of the emerging Greek society.

Aside from fictional works, the Greek Dark Ages, spanning from roughly the 12th to the 9th century BCE, was an enigmatic period characterized by a significant cultural and economic hiatus. This essentially began with the fading of the grandeur of the Mycenaean civilization. Renowned for its palatial centers, military prowess, and sophisticated culture, the rapid and perplexing fall of Mycenae, one of the most prominent of these centers, was a loss to the region.

At the zenith of its power during the Late Bronze Age, Mycenae, situated on the Peloponnese peninsula, stood as a symbol of Mycenaean strength and wealth. Its cyclopean walls, magnificent palace complexes, and intricate engineering bore testimony to the architectural, engineering, and organizational skills of this civilization. Sadly, with the waning of the Mycenaean civilization, their famed bastions like Mycenae and Pylos crumbled into obscurity.

Along with the physical decay of the Mycenaean culture, there was an economic and intellectual faltering as well. Elaborate trade networks fractured, and the production and exportation of Mycenaean crafts, particularly their pottery, ceased. Essentially, the Aegean region moved from a centralized, palace-based economy to a more localized subsistence. Furthermore, the Linear B writing system was largely abandoned, resulting in a dearth of written records from this period. With few primary sources, historians must rely on archaeological evidence alone to reconstruct this chapter of Greek history.

Yet, even as the current writing system faltered, a new one was gradually shaped during the Greek Dark Ages. The Greek alphabet, partially influenced by Linear B and deeply inspired by the Phoenician alphabet, began to take shape. The evolving Greek script, incorporating vowels and consonants, laid the foundation for written Greek communication.

The power vacuum left by the Mycenaeans opened the door for the rise of new populations, chiefly the Dorians. This precipitated massive population shifts and increased cultural diversity as the Dorians brought with them their languages, customs, and traditions. Furthermore, the establishment of new settlements that would grow to be influential city centers like Sparta occurred at this time.

With the increased localization of the Greek Dark Ages, the foundation of the *polis*, or Greek city-state, began to take form. The Mycenaeans' palatial centers were usually governed by a ruler who held centralized authority over an extensive territory; however, with the fall of Mycenae, there was a fracturing of both territory and power. New forms of political organization began on a hyper-local level, and the result was a large number of independent city-states. These *poleis* (plural for *polis*) later became the bedrock of Greek political and social life.

One of the defining features of the *polis* was its autonomy. Each city-state was self-governing and had its own political institutions, laws, and forms of governance. This diversity was reflected in the various political structures, including monarchies, oligarchies, and democracies. Additionally, the sudden appearance of multiple small city centers heralded the rise of urbanization in the Aegean region. The heart of a *polis* was its *agora*, a central square or marketplace where civic, political, and social activities converged. The *agora* became the focal point of a city's public life, serving as a space for trade, politics, and cultural exchange. Unique traditions, religious practices, festivals, and more sprang up in the various *poleis*, fostering a sense of local identity.

Naturally, as humans often do, these Ancient Greeks developed an affinity for and loyalty to their home city-states. Citizenship in a *polis* was a defining aspect of a person's identity in Ancient Greece. To be a citizen was to have certain rights and responsibilities, including participation in the political life of the city-state. However, citizenship was typically restricted to free, adult males only, and it was considered a privilege that came with civic duties.

The autonomy and diversity of individual *poleis* often led to rivalries and conflicts. City-states would form alliances or engage in political and military battles for regional dominance. These sometimes led to bloody and protracted conflicts that will be discussed in later chapters.

In the end, the very notion of a "Dark Age" is challenged by the archaeological record. In the 1980s, gravesites were uncovered dating to around 1000 BCE on the island of Euboea off the Attic peninsula. A notable discovery in the village of Lefkandi was a mausoleum that revealed signs of wealth, prestige, and trade connections with foreign nations. Lefkandi boasts a double burial site of a man and a woman. The ashes are stored in bronze receptacles from Cyprus, and the woman, in particular, is interred with gold items that are stunning and intricate in their design. Additionally, artifacts linked to Egypt were found, and both individuals were interred alongside horses. Furthermore, the style of the mausoleum is similar in design to later Greek temples.

In a time when Greek civilization was thought to be isolated and impoverished, the site at Lefkandi refutes this. However, without more sources, it is difficult to know if Lefkandi was an outlier.

Nevertheless, the Greek Dark Ages laid the cornerstone for the subsequent Archaic and Classical Periods of Greek history. The Greek alphabet and city-state emerged during this transformative era, while Mycenaean legacy was kept alive through oral narratives and epic poems. While termed a "Dark Age," it was more akin to the darkness of a nurturing womb or freshly cultivated land rather than the darkness of demise and burial. The fruitful blossoms of Greek civilization would sprout from the seeds of the Greek Dark Ages.

2

THE POWER OF THE POLIS: A BROAD LOOK AT THE ARCHAIC PERIOD (C. 800–C. 500 BCE)

I f the typical narrative about Greek history is to be believed, the Greek Dark Ages gradually yielded to the light of a new era. However, as has already been noted, history is rarely so neat, and transitions are rarely so clean. Instead, it is a ragged, gradual growth forward that enables historians to divide the bygone eras into digestible chunks. Said to be between 800 and 500 BCE, the Archaic Period witnessed the rise of Greek culture, the differentiation of city-states, and the dawn of various artistic, political, and intellectual innovations.

Though Greeks were already present in Anatolia, the beginning of the Archaic Period was marked by a large number of new Greek settlements springing up outside the geographical bounds of the Greek peninsulas and islands. It is worth noting that when discussing the

Archaic Greeks, the term "colonization" does not have the same connotations that later states like the Roman and British empires lend the word. This was not a conscious, state-sponsored effort to expand Greek dominion throughout the Mediterranean. Instead, it was a weapon employed to combat various problems. Pushed by need and curiosity rather than purely expansionist ambitions, the Archaic Greeks established various colonies and trading posts throughout the Mediterranean and Black Sea regions.

The drive of the Greek city-states to colonize during this era stemmed from multiple factors. In the past, it has been posited that overpopulation and the strain on agricultural resources in the city-states created a pressing need for new settlements. Colonization offered a solution by providing an outlet for surplus populations and reducing the pressure on arable land. However, in recent times, this has largely been rejected since there is no sound evidence to support a population boom in Greece at this time, and the early colonial expeditions were few–hardly enough to make a dent in a swelling population. Furthermore, other means of population control were already in use during the Archaic Period, such as rudimentary forms of contraception or the more gruesome option of infanticide.

Political and social dynamics within the city-states, including internal strife and political tensions, played a crucial role in driving colonization, as did economic incentives. Individuals and groups sought fresh opportunities abroad for various reasons, ranging from expanding influence and addressing domestic instability to the pursuit of economic prospects. Many city-states endorsed colonization as a multi-faceted strategy that catered to these diverse motivations. As a result, colonies often emerged as vibrant trade hubs, accessing valuable resources like metals, timber, and agricultural products, while also serving as outlets for political and social ambitions.

This tale unfolded across a broad region, and though many different city-states participated, it was primarily led by the Euboean Greeks in the early days. As a reminder, Euboean Greeks inhabited the island of Euboea, a large land mass off the coast of the Attic peninsula. The primacy of the Euboeans over other Greeks is born out in the archaeological record, with Euboean pottery discovered across various sites. It is also present in the written historical record, most notably supported by the work of Livy, a Roman historian born in the 1st century BCE.

In the Western Mediterranean, Greeks established colonies in the southern parts of Italy and France, a region later dubbed *Magna Graecia* by the Romans. Notable settlements emerged, including Sybaris, founded by the Achaeans and Troezenians (Troezen); Syracuse, founded by the Corinthians (Corinth); and Massalia (known today

as Marseille), established by the Phocaeans (Pho-
caea/Phokaia).

To the east, Greek colonies extended beyond the Mediterranean coast of Asia Minor and up into the interior,
crawling along the Black Sea coast, particularly in the
Pontic region. Cities such as Byzantium (later known as
Constantinople and then Istanbul), founded by settlers
from the Attic city of Megara, and Olbia, founded by
Ionians from Miletus, thrived as vital colonial outposts. In
North Africa, a group of settlers from the Cycladic island
of Thera (presently referred to as Santorini) established
the city of Cyrene, situated in present-day Libya, and a
contingent of Milesians (Miletus) founded the small
trading station of Naukratis in Egypt.

The impacts of Greek colonization were multi-faceted. A
significant cultural exchange occurred as Greek colonists
introduced their language, art, and traditions to local
populations. This interaction led to a rich cross-pollination of cultures and left an enduring imprint on the development of the Mediterranean. Economically, colonies
blossomed into bustling centers of trade and commerce,
enriching both their mother cities and the colonies themselves. This economic prosperity, in turn, contributed to
the affluence and prestige of the Greek city-states.

Politically, the outcomes varied: while some colonies
eventually evolved into independent city-states, others
maintained strong ties to their mother cities. The nature

of these relationships fluctuated, but colonies frequently played significant roles in shaping the political dynamics of their respective regions.

Greek colonies displayed distinctive organizational structures. They often mirrored the governance systems of their founders' city-states, embracing the framework of the *polis*. Within these colonies, independent councils, laws, and civic institutions were established, reflecting the city-state model. However, governance was not uniform, and a notable characteristic was the prevalence of oligarchies in some colonies. Here, power was concentrated within a select group of elite families, shaping the political landscape differently from their parent city-states.

By the late 6th century BCE, the fervor of colonization began to wane, influenced in part by the presence of already well-established colonies and shifting political dynamics within Greece. Nevertheless, the legacy of Greek colonization was enduring. This exchange of ideas and practices provided fertile ground for the subsequent flourishing of art, philosophy, and science, marking a significant contribution to the collective heritage of human civilization.

Even though the early seeds of the *polis* were sewn during the preceding Dark Age, it should be remembered that many of the Greek city-states were still in their nascent stages. Some of the city-states that founded colonies were barely established themselves. For example, the city-state of Corinth was just taking form when it founded Syracuse on the island of Sicily in 733 BCE.

Nevertheless, as the Archaic Period progressed, many city-states underwent *synoikismos*, or "gathering together." Essentially, this could mean two things. In the first, the population of a specific region started to gather and develop urban centers in a centralized location. In the second, despite the population staying spread out, they still achieved some form of political cohesion. This process happened over time, with the physical and the political unification often occurring at different times or, in some cases, not at all. To illustrate, the city-state of Athens was eventually synoecized many years after its initial political unification. At the same time, Sparta remained physically spread out, refusing to gather behind city walls like their Athenian counterparts.

It is thought that the first indication that a region was beginning to undergo physical *synoikismos* was the erection of some sort of sanctuary. These were usually temples dedicated to various gods. While these may have started as smaller buildings, some, like the Acropolis in Athens, ballooned into large, elaborate temple complexes dedicated to a specific god or goddess. However, the presence of a sanctuary isn't enough to indicate the development of a *polis*. Some sanctuaries were constructed in remote areas, and urban centers did not rise around them.

No matter the underlying reasons, various territories began to define and establish political and geographic borders during the centuries of the Archaic Period. Notable ones include Athens, Sparta, Corinth, and Megara. As mentioned in the previous chapter, these areas developed along different pathways and ended up with separate governments, attitudes, and economic outcomes. Even areas that were geographically quite close experienced a diversity of governments. Athens and Corinth are a little over fifty miles apart, and both city-states grew prosperous in their own right. However, the democratic system of government eventually laid out by the Athenians was a far cry from the oligarchy pursued by their Corinthian neighbors.

If all of this sounds a bit vague, that's because it is. There are scant sources of satisfactory caliber to characterize the political development of Archaic Greece properly. Much of what is known to posterity has been passed down through the filtered lens of Greece's later Classical scholars, and a good bit of what survives focuses specifically on Athenian development. Much of what is fact, fiction, or cultural hyperbole is lost to the sands of time. One can look at Classical Greece and deduce that its social and governmental structure grew out of Archaic Greece. However, knowing where and when specific cultural and political mores appeared is difficult. Moreover, many renowned Greeks from this era are likely either fictional representations or a composite of various individuals and concepts merged into a singular figure.

Two examples can be pointed to: Lycurgus of Sparta and Solon of Athens. Lycurgus, whose existence was questioned even in days of antiquity, is the reputed architect of Sparta's unique way of life. His story, a blend of myth and history, paints a vivid portrait of a society that would become the stuff of legend. Lycurgus, as the tale goes, was the visionary behind the Spartan constitution. He is said to have traveled far and wide, learning from diverse legal systems before returning to Sparta to establish a foundational set of laws known as the "Great Rhetra." This body of laws laid the groundwork for the dual kingship, the *gerousia* (a council of elders), and the *apella* (an assembly of citizens). Spartan society was reshaped around these principles.

Lycurgus's influence was felt in the pursuit of equality among Spartan citizens. Note that the word "citizens" is important; Spartans are not remembered for strongly egalitarian values regarding those they viewed as outsiders. His reforms aimed to minimize disparities in wealth, promoting a Spartan way of life marked by simplicity and frugality. Spartan citizens were bound to a communal ideal, and conspicuous displays of wealth were discouraged. The hallmark of Lycurgus's Sparta was its formidable military prowess. Boys in Sparta underwent grueling physical and military training from an early age. Lycurgus's vision prioritized physical fitness, combat readiness, and the instillation of unwavering discipline.

Remarkably, Lycurgus's reforms extended to women in Spartan society, which was unusual among the largely patriarchal Greek *poleis*. While they didn't partake in military training, they were encouraged to engage in physical fitness and intellectual pursuits. This unique approach allowed Spartan women a degree of independence and influence that set them apart from their counterparts in other Greek city-states.

In the end, Lycurgus's historical authenticity remains shrouded in uncertainty. Whether he was a flesh-and-blood historical figure or more of a mythical construct is a matter of debate. The blend of historical fact and legend in his story makes it challenging to discern the precise boundaries of his influence. Regardless of the historicity of Lycurgus, his legacy endures in the pages of history. The Spartan society he is associated with has left an indelible mark on the ancient world. It was a society characterized by its martial ethos, communal values, and the creation of some of the most disciplined and effective soldiers of antiquity.

On the other side of the coin is Solon of Athens. His historicity, unlike that of Lycurgus, is not questioned. He is undoubtedly a real figure whose fragments of written works have survived into the modern era. However, what can be entirely attributed to him and what was later assigned to him by Athenian politicians, historians, and citizens remains in question. Born into an aristocratic family around 638 or 630 BCE, he rose to prominence during a period of profound social and political upheaval in the city-state.

The Athens of Solon's era grappled with economic inequality and strife between the aristocracy, known as the *Eupatridae*, and the common people, comprised of the *Geomori* (landowners) and *Demiurgi* (artisans and merchants). In response to these challenges, Solon was appointed as a mediator to bring stability and fairness to the city. Solon's legacy is rooted in his transformative reforms, known as the *Seisachtheia*, or the "shaking off of burdens." His measures aimed at alleviating the plight of the lower classes and curbing the power of the aristocracy.

One of his most striking acts was the cancellation of all debts, freeing those who had been enslaved due to indebtedness. This move was a crucial step toward relieving the burden on the common people. Solon restructured the Athenian economy by regulating weights and measures, encouraging trade, and promoting the cultivation of cash crops, such as olive trees. These reforms laid the groundwork for a more prosperous Athens.

Solon introduced a novel four-class system based on wealth, known as the "Solonian classes." Each class was endowed with specific rights and responsibilities, with the highest rank, the *pentakosiomedimnoi*, enjoying the most significant political privileges. To belong to the *pentako-siomedimnoi*, a person's land had to generate at least five hundred bushels of corn or equivalent goods per annum. Other classes included the *hippeis*, or knights, whose land produced between three hundred and five hundred bushels. Next came the *zeugitai*, or craftsmen, who produced two hundred to three hundred bushels, and finally, the *thetes*, or laborers. These people worked the land that belonged to the other classes and were responsible for generating less than two hundred bushels annually.

One of Solon's most significant political innovations was the creation of the Council of 400, drawn from the three lower classes. This council was entrusted with advising on legislative matters, thus giving a voice to a broader section of the Athenian population.

While Solon's reforms did not transform Athens into a full-fledged democracy, they ushered in crucial democratic elements. Solon's legacy lies in introducing greater political participation for common citizens and in the foundational principles of justice and moderation in governance. Solon's contributions to Athens were profound. He facilitated the transition from an aristocratic rule to a society marked by democratic ideals. His reforms paved the way for the more radical democratic changes brought about by Cleisthenes and the eventual evolution of Athenian democracy, a hallmark of the city-state that would shape the course of history.

So, as the various Greek city-states began to grow and come into their own during the Archaic Period, another time-honored tradition was initiated. One of the first "recorded" dates in Greek history is 776 BCE, though they likely would have called the year by a different name or number than is recorded by modern humanity. This year is significant to the Greeks because it was the first year the Olympic Games were ever held.

Since the Olympics began chiefly as a religious celebration, it would be appropriate to briefly address the relatively well-known Greek pantheon and religion at this time. It was a complex polytheistic system that revolved around a panoply of gods and goddesses who played central roles in the lives of the Greeks. These deities were believed to inhabit the natural world and control various aspects of human existence. The most prominent gods and goddesses included Zeus, the king of the gods; Hera, his queen; Apollo, the god of the sun; Artemis, Apollo's twin and the goddess of the hunt; Athena, the goddess of war and wisdom; Demeter, the goddess of the harvest; Dionysus, the god of fertility, wine, and pleasure; Poseidon, the god of the sea; and Hades, the god of the underworld.

Religious practices were a fundamental part of daily life in Ancient Greece, and rituals, festivals, and sacrifices were conducted to appease and honor the gods. Temples, like the Parthenon in Athens, served as places of worship and were filled with statues and offerings to the deities. The ancient Greeks also believed in fate, with oracles like the Oracle of Delphi providing divine guidance and predictions.

The historical origins of the Olympics, a sporting spectacle of enduring legacy, offer a complex narrative blending myth and reality. Rooted in the heart of Ancient Greece, the Games were steeped in ancient traditions and were a testament to the Greeks' pursuit of physical and spiritual excellence. The fabled birth of the Olympic Games can be traced to ancient Greek mythology, where they were attributed to the mighty deity Zeus. According to the myth, Heracles (the Greek name for Hercules), one of the greatest Greek heroes, initiated the Games in honor of his father, Zeus. This divine connection would underscore the sacred nature of the Olympics.

As mentioned above, the earliest documented Olympic Games, recorded by the 5th century BCE Greek historian Hippias of Elis, date to 776 BCE. Held in Olympia, they emerged first as a regional festival within the larger context of Panhellenic events. The first Olympic victor was Coroebus, who won the only event: a 192-meter footrace.

The chosen site of Olympia, nestled in the western Peloponnese, held a special place in the ancient Greek world.

It would later become the home of the temple of Zeus, the sacred altar of Pelops, and the great statue of Zeus by Phidias, known as one of the Seven Wonders of the Ancient World. The natural beauty of the region and its serene groves offered an ideal setting for the Games.

In time, the early Olympics grew into more than a mere sporting event; they were a religious festival of profound significance. The contests included foot races, combat sports, and athletic feats like the long jump and discus throw. The *stadion*, a footrace of just under 200 meters, was particularly prestigious. Athletes were typically soldiers, though they could be anyone from farmers to nobles. These participants often competed unclothed, hoping to reflect the ideal of the Greek body. Women were barred from competing and attending but could win Olympic wreaths through a technicality. In chariot races, the owner of the chariot, rather than the driver, was declared the winner, and women could own chariots. As a result, a Spartan princess, Kyniska, won two Olympic wreaths during the 300s BCE.

Much the same as today, the Olympics were, even from their earliest days, celebrated every four years. They were part of the larger Panhellenic Games. The other three events were the Pythian Games at Delphi, the Nemean Games at Argolis in Nemea, and the Isthmian Games celebrated on the Isthmus of Corinth. The ancient Greeks used the four years between the Olympics as a measure of time, referring to it as an Olympiad. The Olympics marked the start of an Olympiad, while the Pythian Games occurred two years after the Olympics in Olympiad year three. The Nemean Games and Isthmian Games were held every two years and celebrated at different times during the same year. These were held in Olympiad years two and four. Just like the Olympics were to honor Zeus, the other games were dedicated to a specific deity. The Pythian Games honored Apollo, and the Isthmian Games honored Poseidon. Like the Olympics, the Nemean Games honored Zeus and his son, Heracles.

To facilitate safe travel and participation, the Greeks observed the Olympic Truce, or *Ekecheiria*, which suspended hostilities during the Games—this period of peace emphasized the universal appeal and panhellenic nature of the Olympics. Despite the historical reputation for animosity between the various city-states, the Olympics provided a platform for cultural exchange and camaraderie among Greeks from various *poleis*, transcending regional rivalries. The wreath, awarded to victors, symbolized their connection to Zeus and elevated the Games to a spiritual and transcendent experience.

Much of what is known about the Olympics and Ancient Greece generally comes from archaeological records and artwork. Archaic Greek art marked a significant departure from the stylized forms of the preceding Dark Ages. The earlier era, termed the Geometric Period, derived its name from the precise geometric designs and detailed patterns adorning pottery and vases. These patterns, featuring circles, zigzags, and meandering lines, showcased the era's methodical spirit. Associated with funerary art, Geometric vases and ceramic grave markers (*kraters*) paid tribute to the departed with funerary scenes and abstract motifs. The Geometric Era's cultural significance lies in its role as a foundation for the artistic developments of the Archaic and Classical Periods, where a transition to more representational art and naturalistic forms would begin to take shape.

With the Greeks venturing into the Mediterranean on colonization excursions throughout the Archaic period, their engagement with the cultures of the Eastern Mediterranean brought a mélange of artistic and cultural influences. This exchange, particularly with the Phoenician and Egyptian civilizations, introduced intricate patterns and exotic motifs into Greek art, creating a vibrant tapestry of cross-cultural creativity.

With the rise of the Archaic period, artists began venturing into the realm of more naturalistic and lifelike portrayals of the human form. Notable among these were the *kouros* (male) and *kore* (female) statues, which embodied youthful figures characterized by their enigmatic smiles, almond-shaped eyes, and an enduring sense of idealized beauty. However, this was not yet the sculptural zenith of Ancient Greece. These *kouros* and *kore* were often stiff in posture, lacking the grace, balance, and movement that later Greek art would exhibit.

The earliest example known is the Sounion *Kouros*[1], which dates to around 600 BCE. Often carved in marble or limestone and used at temples and grave sites, Egyptian art likely heavily influenced the kouros and kore, showcasing the same geometry, idealization, and perfection within the stiff, unnatural posing. However, this style was not stagnant—evolution can be found as the decades passed. About 100 years after the Sounion *Kouros*, the Aristodikos *Kouros*[2] was carved. Though the subject matter remains the same—a healthy and athletic young male—the musculature and shape of the body are far more realistic. Additionally, though the pose remains the same, there is a subtle weight shift and s-curve to the body, making it appear slightly more lifelike.

Sculpture was a cornerstone of Archaic Greek art. These sculptures often served as votive offerings and commemorative tributes, unveiling the early Greeks' fascination with the human physique. Aside from their sculptural talents, Archaic Greece was renowned for its mastery of pottery, and this period saw an efflorescence of vase painting. The pottery often came in many shapes, like vases, dishes, and amphorae. An amphora is a specific type of ancient Greek pottery vessel with two handles and a narrow neck. It was commonly used for storing and transporting liquids, such as wine and oil.

The striking techniques of black-figure and red-figure pottery, with either its black silhouettes and intricate red detailing or red figures with black detailing, are instantly recognizable. The exquisite Attic black-figure and red-figure vases often depicted scenes from mythology, daily life, and athletic contests, creating a canvas of stories in clay. As the name suggests, these originated in ancient Attica and had diverse uses. Often functioning as containers for liquids, they were also employed in religious rituals, served as decorative pieces in homes and public spaces, played a role in trade, and were sometimes placed in tombs as funerary items.

Black-figure and red-figure pottery was popular primarily in the 6th and 5th centuries BCE. In black-figure pottery, the background of the vase was painted black, and the figures were left in the natural color of the clay, usually reddish-orange. Details of the figures were added by incising lines into the black background to reveal the clay beneath, resulting in a sharp contrast. Figures on black-figure vases often appear silhouetted and have a characteristic glossy appearance. Artists had limited means to depict finer details and had to rely on intricate incisions and the use of added colors for ornamentation. The scenes were typically more stylized and less naturalistic. The François Vase[3] and the Exekias Amphora[4] are famous examples of black-figure pottery.

Red-figure pottery reversed the technique and emerged a little after the black-figure. The images and details were painted using a black glaze, while the background was left in the clay's natural red or orange color. This allowed for greater precision and more naturalistic depictions, thus allowing for more fluid and detailed depictions of figures. Artists could now portray facial expressions and anatomical features with greater accuracy, leading to a more life-like and dynamic appearance in the artwork. The Euphronios *Krater*[4] and the Berlin Painter's Amphorae[5] are celebrated examples of red-figure pottery.

Large-scale artwork and architecture were also present during the Archaic Era, with grand temples and architectural marvels being constructed. Temples played a central role in Ancient Greece's religious and architectural landscape, serving as venues for religious rituals, ceremonies, and festivals. They were also important centers of civic and community life. These temples, central to worship and home to statues of gods and goddesses, were among the culture's pivotal institutions. They vividly showcased the evolving architectural styles and artistic sensibilities of the era. Each temple was dedicated to a specific deity, such as Athena, Apollo, or Hera, and the cult statue housed within would represent that deity.

In the Archaic Period, Greek temples embraced the dominant architectural style known as the Doric order. These temples exuded a sense of simplicity, marked by robust columns that stood firm, eschewing ornate embellishments. The columns, often fluted with distinct grooves, supported an entablature comprising a plain architrave and a frieze adorned with *metopes*. These rectangular panels were often carved with intricate relief sculptures. The pediment formed a triangular gable at the temple's summit, serving as a canvas to display sculptural artistry. These sculptures depicted mythological narratives, heroic deeds, and scenes from Greek history. The Archaic Period witnessed the transition from rigid and stylized sculpture to more naturalistic and dynamic forms. Figures on early Archaic pediments tended to be quite stiff in manner, but as the period progressed, the sculptural style became more fluid and expressive.

Within the temple's core, called the *cella* or *naos*, resided the sacred statue of the deity to whom the temple was devoted. This inner sanctum was frequently subdivided, adding two distinct chambers: the *pronaos*, positioned at the front, and the *opisthodomos*, found at the rear. The *cella's* roof, a marvel of construction, was usually crafted from sturdy wooden beams and shielded by terracotta tiles.

The Archaic temples featured one of two primary architectural designs. Peripteral temples showcased a solitary row of columns enveloping the *cella*. In contrast, pseudoperipteral temples embraced an inner and an outer row of columns encircling the *cella*, thus yielding a more expansive and inviting interior space. The Parthenon in Athens is a well-known example of a peripteral temple, while the Temple of Olympian Zeus at Agrigento is a solid specimen of a pseudoperipteral temple. However, it should be noted that neither of these structures were constructed during the Archaic Period; they date back to the 400s BCE and are products of the early Classical Period.

The Archaic Period laid the groundwork for the evolution of Greek temple architecture into the Classical Period. The transition from the Archaic to the Classical Era saw a shift toward greater refinement and sophistication in architectural design and in the sculptures used to adorn the temples. The Classical Period would produce some of the most iconic Greek temples, such as the Parthenon in Athens. Yet, the Archaic Era also produced well-known and enduring temples like the Temple of Hera at Olympia and the Temple of Artemis in Corcyra (present-day Corfu).

Beyond just architecture, the artistry of the Archaic Period was a stepping stone to the Classical Era, setting the stage for the artistic techniques and concepts that would reach their zenith in the centuries to come. The innovations and pioneering spirit of this period laid the groundwork for the timeless masterpieces of the Classical Age that continue to captivate people centuries later.

The art of Archaic Greece unveils a canvas of creativity and evolving aesthetics, where experimentation and inspiration converged to paint a vivid cultural portrait. These artistic achievements continue to beguile, illuminating Ancient Greece's cultural and aesthetic essence.

As the Archaic Age drew to a close, Greece had moved beyond its borders, instituted an alphabet, constructed glorious temples, and much more. Time-honored traditions were formed, and a cultural aesthetic was born. Yet, each city-state remained insular, fiercely independent, and ready to compete for dominance in the region. The next chapter will explore the specifics of various *poleis* in more detail.

3

POLITICAL INTRIGUE AND WAR IN THE ARCHAIC AGE (C. 800–C. 500 BCE)

The Archaic Period in Ancient Greece was a time of political experimentation, social evolution, and emerging conflicts between various city-states. Though they shared geographical, historical, cultural, linguistic, and religious ties, the various *poleis* still couldn't seem to work together cohesively. Yet, a threat was looming on the horizon, and the Greek city-states couldn't afford to remain so glibly individualistic for much longer. The most well-remembered city-states are, naturally, Athens and Sparta, but other territories like Corinth, Thebes, Miletus, Eretria, and Chalcis will be discussed in this chapter, as well.

Before delving into individual city-states, it is worthwhile to deliberate on a few of the notable individuals who were prominent in the early shaping of Greece. The Seven Sages of Greece, also known as the Seven Wise Men, were a group of renowned individuals from Ancient Greece who lived during the 6th century BCE. They were celebrated for their wisdom and contributions to various fields, including philosophy, ethics, and governance. The identity of the Seven Sages may vary slightly in different lists, but the following individuals are commonly recognized as members: Thales of Miletus, Solon of Athens, Pittacus of Mytilene, Bias of Priene, Cleobulus of Lindos, Periander of Corinth, and Chilon of Sparta. Other names that sometimes appear on the list are Myson of Chenae and Anacharsis the Scythian.

Thales of Miletus is often regarded as the first philosopher in the Western tradition. He was a mathematician, astronomer, and thinker who sought to explain natural phenomena through rational, non-mythological means. Thales' focus on natural explanations laid the groundwork for the development of Greek philosophy. Solon, discussed in the previous chapter, was an Athenian statesman and lawmaker. He is known for introducing a series of legal and political reforms in Athens to address social and economic inequalities. His contributions to Athenian democracy and law had a lasting impact.

Pittacus of Mytilene was a military leader and statesman from the island of Lesbos. He is remembered for his wisdom and practical advice and is often quoted for sayings on moderation and self-control. His leadership and contributions to political stability were highly regarded. While Bias of Priene was also known for his ethical and moral aphorisms, he emphasized fairness, justice, and the importance of virtue. His wisdom contributed to the development of Greek ethics and moral philosophy.

Cleobulus of Lindos was a philosopher and poet. Like many other sages, he is credited with aphorisms promoting moderation, temperance, and self-control. His sayings served as guidelines for personal conduct. Periander of Corinth was a prominent statesman and ruler of Corinth. He was known for his achievements in governance and is remembered for his contributions to Corinth's prosperity and political stability. Finally, Chilon of Sparta was a statesman and one of the *ephors*, a group of elected officials in the Spartan government. He emphasized the virtues of self-discipline and self-control, which were highly valued in Spartan society.

The significance of the Seven Sages of Greece is underscored by their collective wisdom and the multifaceted arenas in which they made their profound contributions. These sages laid the intellectual foundations for Western philosophy and ethics. They offered practical guidance to individuals and leaders through their aphorisms and maxims, emphasizing moderation, justice, and self-control. Their profound influence reverberated throughout the development of political and legal systems, fostering the stability and progress of Greek city-states.

Moreover, their teachings and writings continued to shape subsequent generations of philosophers, thinkers, and leaders, thereby molding the trajectory of Greek thought and, by extension, Western intellectual tradition. The Seven Sages bequeathed an enduring legacy of wisdom and ethical principles, a legacy that played a pivotal role in the intellectual and moral evolution of Ancient Greece and the broader world.

Athens, the main city of Attica, emerged as a city-state of profound influence and dynamic transformation. The city ultimately became known during the Classical Period as a democratic stronghold and a crucible of artistic and philosophical innovation—this was all made possible by the choices established during this era by various Athenian forefathers.

Two such forefathers were Solon and another luminary named Cleisthenes. Solon, as discussed in the last chapter, initiated significant reforms aimed at mitigating the economic and social disparities that had troubled the city. If Solon laid the groundwork for Athenian democracy, Cleisthenes saw it to fruition. However, prior to the rise of Cleisthenes, the city-state was governed by a series of tyrants. The Athenian tyrants were rulers who, as the name suggests, ruled autocratically. They are distinct from the typical image of tyrants as oppressive rulers, as many implemented reforms and were regarded as some-what benevolent autocrats. Notable among them were Peisistratus and his son Hippias. Peisistratus was renowned for his progressive policies, whereas his son Hippias, although initially adopting similar measures, ultimately governed with greater oppression. Their rule set the stage for the transition to Athenian democracy, with the pivotal role played by Cleisthenes in political reforms.

As a decisive figure in ancient Athens, Cleisthenes is often celebrated as the "Father of Athenian Democracy." He was not a tyrant but an *archon*—a high-ranking magistrate in the Athenian government—during the reign of Hippias, and a member of the wealthy noble Alcmaeonid family. He lived during the late 6th century BCE and played a transformative role in shaping the political landscape of Athens. His reforms were instrumental in the evolution of the Athenian political system from an oligarchy to a more democratic model.

Primarily known for his efforts to expand political participation, Cleisthenes introduced a series of groundbreaking reforms that aimed to break the influence of the powerful aristocratic families, like his own, the Alcmaeonids. His goal was to create and promote a more inclusive form of governance. Cleisthenes restructured the Athenian population into ten new tribes, known as *demes*, based on geographical regions and proximity rather than ancient ancestral ties. This change reduced the dominance of traditional kinship networks in favor of regional identity and participation in the political process.

He expanded the *Boule*, or council of 400, to 500 members, ensuring a representative body composed of fifty citizens from each of the ten tribes. This council met almost daily and played a crucial role in preparing legislation and agendas for the assembly (*ekklesia*), making the legislative process more democratic. As an aside, the *ekklesia* was the primary assembly of citizens in ancient Athens and was a cornerstone of their democratic system. Comprising all eligible male citizens, the *ekklesia* met regularly to discuss and vote on important matters of state, such as legislation, decrees, and political appointments. The *ekklesia* was not a uniquely Athenian institution. Many of the Greek city-states had something similar within their governmental frameworks.

Other principles Cleisthenes championed were *isonomia*, or equal participation in governance, and *isegoria*, or the equal right to speak in the *ekklesia*. This ushered in a broader and more equitable participation of citizens in the political discourse of the city.

Though Cleisthenes' democratic reforms laid the groundwork for the Athenian democracy that would later flourish during the Classical Period, his legacy extended far beyond Athens. His ideas on democracy and political equality inspired subsequent political thinkers, including the founders of numerous modern democracies. His work set a precedent for the idea that a government should derive its authority from the consent and participation of its citizens. This idea continues, centuries later, to be echoed in the present day.

Governmental and political developments aside, the Archaic Period also witnessed a cultural renaissance within Athens. Athens' reputation as a bastion of artistry and intellectualism took root during this time. The city-state became a vibrant center of artistic and literary endeavors. Athens put forth a concerted effort to host various poetic, musical, and literary activities, fostering creativity and cultural exchange among their citizens and visitors. The construction of the Acropolis, which would later become an iconic symbol of Ancient Greece, commenced during this time. Black-figure and red-figure pottery, a distinctively Athenian innovation, displayed remarkable craftsmanship and narrative flair.

The Archaic Period was a transformative chapter in the Athenian story, paving the way for the city's remarkable journey. This era's political developments, artistic achievements, and cultural innovation became the cornerstones of Athens' identity. They served as the foundation for the city's enduring legacy, which would continue to flourish in the Classical Period and define the course of Western civilization. In the Archaic Period, Athens was a city-state on the precipice of monumental change. Its embrace of democracy, vibrant cultural landscape, and pivotal role in facing external threats solidified its status as a beacon of Greek civilization, an identity it would wear proudly in the following centuries.

On the other side of the coin resided pugnacious Sparta. In the heart of the Peloponnese, this distinctive and formidable city-state was renowned for its unwavering commitment to military excellence and the extraordinary discipline of its citizens. During the Archaic Period, Spartans developed a society that diverged significantly from the democratic ideals of Athens and deeply valued strength, discipline, and military supremacy.

The unique constitution supposedly established by the legendary lawgiver Lycurgus lay at the core of Spartan society. It aimed to create a society entirely dedicated to producing exceptional warriors. The constitution divided citizens into classes, with the Spartan citizens, known as *Spartiates*, forming the warrior elite. Beneath them were the *Perioeci*, free residents, artisans, and farmers who performed essential functions. Many *Perioeci* were the original residents of the Peloponnesian peninsula, the Achaeans (Mycenaeans). They paid taxes and served in the army but had little political agency. Lastly were the *helots*, a slave class responsible for agriculture. *Helots*, often obtained through conquest, included Achaeans who had opposed the Doric Spartans during their expansion across the Peloponnesian peninsula in the Dark Ages.

Central to Spartan life was the *agoge*, an austere and rigorous education and training system. From a young age, Spartan boys were subjected to demanding physical exercise, combat training, and character development. They were taught to endure hardship, adapt to challenging conditions, and, above all, prioritize the welfare and defense of Sparta. Sparta's existence and survival revolved around its military. The city-state's primary objective was the preservation of its warriors' prowess. As a result, Spartans mainly did not engage in agriculture and trade, leaving these tasks to the *perioeci* and *helots*. The warrior class was expected to dedicate their lives wholly to the art of war.

As for the women, as mentioned in the previous chapter, Spartan females enjoyed a degree of freedom and influence uncommon in the ancient world. They were educated and physically trained with the goal of producing healthy and strong offspring for the Spartan army. This emphasis on women's health and education was rooted in the belief that strong mothers would bear strong sons.

This militaristic focus gave Sparta dominance over the Peloponnesian region, and its ascendency over the peninsula was established during the Archaic Era. One of the first steps in this direction was the First Messenian War (c. 740–720 BCE), where Sparta asserted its dominance over neighboring Messenia. This intense and protracted conflict stemmed from the growing disparity in social and economic conditions, and the war resulted in the eventual subjugation of Messenia by Sparta, marking the Messenians as *helots* and altering the sociopolitical landscape of the Peloponnese. The war was a foundational episode in Spartan history, contributing to the formation of their military state and the consolidation of their power in the region. It will be revisited in the latter half of this chapter.

Sparta's reputation as a martial powerhouse was widely acknowledged, and it often served as a symbol of Greek valor to the broader Mediterranean world. However, its inflexible societal structure and focus on military preparedness left it somewhat isolated, particularly compared to the political and intellectual developments in Athens. In the Archaic Period, Sparta was a city-state that embraced an extreme and highly structured way of life. It upheld the values of soldierly skill, discipline, and self-sacrifice as the highest of virtues. While its approach differed markedly from the democratic and intellectual dynamism of Athens, Sparta's dedication to military excellence was impressive in its own right.

Located on a narrow isthmus between Athens and Sparta, Corinth was a prosperous maritime city-state with tremendous strategic and economic importance. Nestled on the tapered stretch of land connecting the Peloponnesian peninsula with mainland Greece, Corinth thrived as a crossroads of trade, innovation, and cultural exchange.

Its location was pivotal to its success. Situated on a vital land bridge that allowed travelers to bypass the treacherous sea voyage around the Peloponnese, the city's two ports, Lechaeum to the west and Cenchreae to the east, facilitated trade and enriched the *polis*.

As a result, throughout the Archaic Period, trade became the lifeblood of Corinth. The city's merchants were renowned throughout the ancient world, conducting commerce with regions as distant as Egypt and Italy. Corinthian traders established colonies and outposts in places like the northern Greek island of Corcyra (modern Corfu) in the Ionian Sea and Syracuse on the Italian island of Sicily, further expanding their economic influence.

Corinth was not just a hub of commerce but a melting pot of various Mediterranean civilizations. The city's bustling *agora*, or marketplace, was a location where travelers and merchants from different corners of the region intermingled. This cross-pollination of cultures is attributed to Corinth's reputation as a center for culture and academia.

Yet, despite its somewhat Athenian bent towards arts and intellectualism, the Corinthian government did not develop in quite the same manner. Instead, during the Archaic Period, the city-state experienced a series of tyrants who held power with varying degrees of influence. Athens experienced its share of tyrants in the Archaic Age, a common occurrence in that era and region. However, unlike Athens, Corinth did not evolve into a bastion of democratic thought. Many of these tyrants, despite the title, acted in the interest of Corinth and its citizens, focusing on the city-state's betterment rather than solely on personal gain and power. Figures like Cypselus and his son Periander (one of the Seven Sages) might have governed the city with an autocratic hand, but they also promoted trade and prosperity, helping to secure Corinth's standing in the ancient world.

Amidst its economic boom from trade, Corinth undertook colonization, establishing cities and trading outposts in strategic locations. This bolstered its economic and political influence throughout the Mediterranean. The two most well-known, Corcyra (Corfu) and Syracuse, have already been discussed. Those, plus others like Ambracia on Greece's western coast, Potidaea on the Chalcidice peninsula in northern Greece, Leucas (Lefkada) in the Ionian Sea, and Anactorium near the mouth of the Ambracian Gulf bolstered Corinth's presence and furthered its maritime interests.

Though the colonies helped enrich Corinth, they did not solely belong to the city-state. Many, such as Syracuse and Corcyra, also became city-states in their own right. A few Corinthian colonies, such as Anactorium and potentially Leucas, were co-founded with settlers from Corcyra, one of Corinth's earliest colonies. As a result, political relationships between the colonies, their mother city-state of Corinth, and other rival city-states were paramount. Corinth's political landscape was marked by an ever-shifting balance of power, including alliances with other city-states such as Sparta. The city's dynamic politics often mirrored the ebb and flow of its commercial interests.

In the Archaic Period, Corinth was a city-state of exceptional vitality and influence. Its strategic location, flourishing commerce, and cultural vibrancy made it a prominent player on the stage of Ancient Greece. The legacy of Corinth during this era is one of prosperity, innovation, and the enrichment of Greek culture through international exchange.

Moving back from the neck of the Peloponnese and returning to the Attic peninsula, there was Thebes. Nestled in the fertile region of Boeotia just over fifty miles north of Athens, Thebes evolved from an inconspicuous town into a formidable power.

Like their Greek counterparts, Thebes' origins are steeped in legend, often traced back to the legendary hero Cadmus. According to the myth, Cadmus was the son of Agenor, a king of Phoenicia. He was tasked with finding his sister Europa, whom Zeus had abducted in the form of a bull. After an exhaustive search, Cadmus arrived in the region that would later become Thebes. With the aid of the goddess Athena, Cadmus founded the city and established the citadel of Thebes, referred to as "Cadmeia" or "Cadmea" in his honor. He is further credited by the Greek historian Herodotus with introducing the Phoenician alphabet to Greece.

Aside from its founding lore, other stories about the city-state mark it as a site of many struggles, immortalized in various dramatic works. Two great tragic poets of Ancient

Greece, Aeschylus and Sophocles, wrote lengthy plays about some mythological aspects of the Theban city-state. Both men mainly focused on the story of the legendary Theban king, Oedipus, who, in an attempt to escape a prophecy, unwittingly fulfills it by killing his father and marrying his mother. When he discovers the truth, he blinds himself in horror and goes into exile. The story explores the themes of fate, free will, and the inescapability of one's destiny.

Aeschylus wrote *Laius, Oedipus,* and *Seven Against Thebes,* focusing on the story surrounding Oedipus and his family. Of the three, only *Seven Against Thebes* seems to have survived in its entirety. Sophocles' Theban trilogy has better stood the ages, with *Oedipus The King (Oedipus Rex), Oedipus at Colonus,* and *Antigone* all well-read texts in the modern age.

Aside from being a fertile ground for literary inspiration, Thebes was also a prominent member of the Boeotian League, a confederation of Boeotian city-states that emerged around 550 BCE. Boeotia is a region in central Greece bordered by the Gulf of Corinth and Attica to the south and southeast, Phocis to the west, the Gulf of Euboea to the east, and a region called Fthiótis to the north. Boeotia boasts fecund fields and an extremely strategic location. Under Theban leadership, the league provided collective security and cooperation, enabling Thebes to assert its influence in the region. The Boeotian League's military and political influence was pivotal in inter-Greek disputes and conflicts with foreign entities.

To be a power player in the region, Thebes needed a strong military, and the city-state's rise to prominence was closely tied to its military prowess. As a result of this martial success, Thebes experienced a period of dominance in Boeotia and beyond. As mentioned, Thebes often found itself embroiled in conflicts with neighboring city-states, notably Athens and Sparta. The Boeotian city-state's strategic position and considerable assets made it a valuable prize in the more significant geopolitical struggles of the era and into the future.

The final city-state discussed in greater detail is not on the Greek peninsulas or islands. Instead, Miletus is located on the western coast of Anatolia, roughly twenty miles south of the present-day Turkish city of Söke, just near the mouth of the Menderes (Büyük Menderes) River. Though not geographically part of Greece, it became a cosmopolitan hub for the ancient Greeks. Its location on the Ionian coast positioned it as a center for trade, cultural interactions, and intellectual exchange.

Like many ancient metropolises, the origins of the city's founding are unclear. Colonists from the island of Crete likely founded the city. However, its mythical origin attributes the founding to a man named Miletus. Various legends differ, but most agree that this man was the offspring of Apollo, the sun god, and was exiled from the island of Crete by the legendary King Minos. This suggests ties between Miletus and the Minoan civilization that flourished on Crete for some time. Miletus' location along the eastern shore of the Aegean Sea granted it prime access to maritime trade routes, allowing it to thrive as a commercial and naval power. The city was perched at the mouth of the Menderes River, which, at the time, offered a natural harbor for ships and fostered maritime activities.

As a result of their nautical proclivities, Miletus became a prolific colonizer. It established over sixty colonies throughout Anatolia, the Mediterranean, and North Africa, particularly along the coasts of the Black Sea and the Sea of Marmara. Notable communities included Naukratis in Egypt, Abydos on the eastern portion of the Hellespont, Cyzicus on the southern coast of the Sea of Marmara, Sinope (present-day Sinop) on the southern coast of the Black Sea, Olbia on the northern coast of the Black Sea in present-day Ukraine, and Panticapaeum (Pantikapaion) on Crimea's eastern coast. These colonies served as outposts for trade, increasing Miletus' economic reach and cultural influence in the wider Mediterranean world. Their wide array of colonies also created cultural diversity in the city-state, unlike other more insular *poleis*, like Sparta. Miletus became known as a sophisticated center that hosted various ethnic and religious identities.

Aside from a general thirst for wandering, it seems that Milesian citizens were also prone to introspection.

Miletus was pivotal in developing early Greek philosophy, with the city home to renowned thinkers like Thales. Earlier mentioned in the text as one of the Seven Sages of Greece, he is also often hailed as the first Western philosopher. The city also produced Anaximander and Anaximenes, students of Thales and talented thinkers in their own right.

Anaximander proposed that an undefined, boundless substance called the *apeiron* was the source of all things. He expanded on Thales' ideas by introducing the concept of the eternal and infinite, challenging traditional mythological explanations of the world's origins. Anaximenes believed that air (or *aer*) was the primary substance from which everything emerged. He asserted that variations in air density explained different forms of matter, offering a systematic and naturalistic perspective. These early Milesian philosophers laid the foundation for philosophical inquiry into the natural world, setting the stage for the development of later Presocratic thinkers and, eventually, the flourishing of Greek philosophy. Their focus on seeking rational explanations for the natural world marked a significant departure from mythological and religious interpretations, and it is often considered the inception of Western philosophy.

Miletus seemed to be a home for intellectual pursuits, renowned for its philosophical musings and contributions to other academic endeavors. Miletus was also the home of Hecataeus, an ancient Greek historian, geographer, and philosopher. He is celebrated as one of the earliest academics of his kind, known for his groundbreaking work in geography. His treatise, *Periēgēsis*, represented one of the first systematic descriptions of various regions and peoples in the known world. Hecataeus seamlessly merged geographical and historical accounts, bridging the realms of myth and fact. His approach paved the way for integrating geography and history in ancient Greek literature, and his efforts profoundly influenced subsequent generations, especially the works of the prolific historian Herodotus.

Much like the other Greek *poleis*, Miletus featured a dynamic political system. However, it should be noted that concrete evidence about the Milesians' political proclivities is thin, and it is difficult for contemporary scholars to obtain true clarity about political life in Archaic Miletus, especially in the years before 500 BCE. There is a general sense that Miletus began as a monarchy, with power concentrated among a few high-ranking noble families.

Over time, this changed into more of an oligarchic tyranny. While power remained concentrated among a few, it introduced a semblance of democracy by electing those tyrants into power. One of the most famous Milesian tyrants was a man named Thrasybulus. He was a tyrant around the same time that Periander of Corinth ruled, and the two were purportedly allies, with Thrasybulus supposedly giving Periander the brutal advice to remove any person who might threaten his rule. Further-more, according to Herodotus, Thrasybulus was also responsible for ending the long war between Miletus and the kingdom of Lydia by tricking the Lydian king, Alyattes, into suing for peace.

Like many other Greek city-states, Milesians experi-mented with their government, and it is thought they slowly drifted toward democracy. Any further trial and error in Miletus was cut short—the city-state and all the other Greek *poleis* in Anatolia were ultimately absorbed into the expanding Persian Empire during the latter half of the 6th century BCE.

Life among the Greek city-states was hardly peaceable before the looming threat from the east. No Greek city-state existed in isolation. Given the diverse views on governance, as well as the wide range of linguistic, reli-gious, and cultural traditions, these city-states frequently clashed with each other for many reasons.

One early and straightforward motive for conflict was territory. The colonial expansion of the Greek city-states at this time has already been detailed, and this competi-tion for resources in the newly settled areas of Italy, Anatolia, and the Black Sea region often led to discord. Even within the peninsulas and islands of Greece, scrab-bling for territory caused bloodshed—especially in the Archaic Period when the borders and boundaries of the various city-states were in their infancy. One of the earliest examples is the conflict between Messenia and Sparta. These two city-states fought several protracted wars during the Archaic Period.

Keep in mind that the Spartans descended from the Dorian Greeks, who probably migrated into the Peloponnese following Mycenae's decline. On the other hand, most Messenians were Achaean Greeks, the ethnic group of the Mycenaeans. When the Dorians arrived, the indigenous Achaeans probably faced significant losses. There are indications of a decline in the Achaean population during this period, with many leaving the Peloponnese to establish colonies elsewhere.

It should be noted that much of what is known of the first conflict comes from the work of Pausanias, a Greek geographer and historian from the 2nd century CE. Only fragments of the sources that Pausanias cites are available today; thus, much of the factual information surrounding the First Messenian War has been lost to time. The dates supplied by Pausanias are 743 to 724 BCE, and he indicates that the war started due to cattle theft. However, the conflict was probably rooted in longstanding territorial and ethnic tensions between the Spartans and Messenians, as animosity between them was evident. Ultimately, Sparta was victorious over Messenia, resulting in the enslavement of a majority of the Messenian population.

The peace did not last long. With most Messenians now living as *helots* under their Spartan overlords, the Second

Messenian War saw a renewed effort by the Messenians to regain their independence from Spartan rule. The exact dates of the conflict are uncertain, but the consensus is that it began around 660 BCE.

As mentioned above, the war was sparked by the ongoing tensions between the Spartan ruling class and the *helots*, mainly of Messenian descent. The *helots*, an enslaved population, sought to break free from their Spartan oppressors. The Messenians, who had been subjugated since the First Messenian War, saw this as an opportunity to launch a revolt against the Spartans. This was particularly championed by a Messenian leader named Aristomenes. While much of his life is shrouded in myth and legend, he is widely recognized as the leader of the Messenian revolt during the Second Messenian War.

Aristomenes and his forces secured some early successes against the Spartans, inflicting notable defeats. However, the Spartans eventually rallied and regained the upper hand, and the war concluded with a Spartan victory. Once again, the Messenians were subjugated and enslaved, and Spartan control over Messenian territory solidified. However, Messenia was not entirely under Sparta's auspices until around 600 BCE, some sixty years after the outset of the war. Those who survived the conflict were either enslaved as *helots* or scattered in diaspora across the Greek world.

Both the First and Second Messenian Wars played a significant role in shaping Spartan society and reinforcing its reliance on *helots* as an essential component of its labor force. It also buttressed Spartan military prowess and furthered their dominance in the Peloponnese. Sparta's quest for more territory continued throughout the Archaic Period, bringing the city-state into conflict with other neighboring entities like Argolis and Arcadia. Sparta's desire for expansion persisted over time, posing challenges for the entire Greek peninsula later in the Classical Period.

Beyond just the desire for territory, city-states also argued over trade. The Lelantine War was a conflict driven by a dispute over colonies and trading that occurred in the late 8th and early 7th century BCE between two ancient Greek city-states, Chalcis and Eretria, both located in Euboea in the Aegean Sea.

Before the conflict, it appears that Chalcis and Eretria worked together, even jointly founding the colony of Cumae near present-day Naples in Italy. What ultimately caused relations between Chalcis and Eretria to sour is not entirely clear. However, it greatly divided the Greek world, pulling various other city-states into alliances against one another. Corinth, Sámos, and Thessaly sided with Chalcis, while Megara and Miletus allied with Eretria. The involvement of the city-states of Erythrae and Chios is uncertain, but they are thought to have joined with Chalcis and Eretria, respectively.

The Lelantine War is one of the earliest recorded instances of sustained conflict between two Greek city-states, and it provides valuable insights into the evolving nature of warfare and territorial disputes in the early Greek world. It was a protracted conflict, drawn out over many years, featuring battles on land and sea. Still, the outcome of the war is somewhat ambiguous, with ancient sources providing different accounts. It is possible that the conflict ended in a stalemate without one city-state decisively defeating the other. The Lelantine War is significant for its role in early Greek history, offering insights into the dynamics of interstate conflicts and territorial disputes in the Archaic Period.

A more ominous force was gathering to the east despite the internal squabbling. In the 6th century BCE, the Persian Empire, under the leadership of Cyrus the Great and his successors, embarked on a remarkable period of expansion and conquest that would shape the history of the ancient world. When Cyrus the Great came into power, the Persian Empire was not the behemoth it would later be, and it is Cyrus who is credited as the founder of the massive Achaemenian Empire. The name "Achaemenian" (or "Achaemenid") is derived from Cyrus's family lineage, which claimed descent from a figure named Achaemenes, whose actual existence is uncertain. It is also referred to as the First Persian Empire, distinct from the Second Persian Empire, or the Sassanid (Sasanian) Empire, a political entity from 224 to 651 CE.

With no massive empire to speak of initially, Cyrus seized the Medes (Media) empire by overthrowing his grandfather, Astyages, around 550 BCE. This land covered significant parts of what is now northwestern Iran and Azerbaijan. Afterward, he set about consolidating his power by uniting the various Iranian tribes in the region before expanding. Meanwhile, to the west, the ruler of the Anatolian kingdom of Lydia, Croesus, was eagerly encroaching on Cyrus' Median territory after hearing of his grandfather's demise.

As a result, Cyrus marched on Lydia, seizing the capital, Sardis, sometime between 547 and 546 BCE. With the Persian takeover of Lydia, all of Asia Minor and the Ionian Greek city-states, which had been vassal states of the Lydian kingdom, fell into Cyrus' hands. Cyrus and his successors weren't satisfied with just settling the score against the Lydians. When Cambyses II and Darius I ascended to the Achaemenid throne, they actively expanded Persian influence. The shadow of Persian ambition began to loom ominously over Greece.

4

THE PROBLEM WITH PERSIA
(522–449 BCE)

C ambyses II was primarily preoccupied with conquering Egypt and expanding into Africa during his rule. This meant that the Greeks experienced a brief respite from Persian attention. However, in 522 BCE, Cambyses II unexpectedly died in Syria while returning to Persia from Egypt. With the throne in peril, Darius, a member of Cambyses II's royal guard and from a side branch of the Achaemenid royal lineage, rushed back to Persia. He discovered that Bardiya, the younger brother of Cambyses II (also known as "Smerdis" in Herodotus' writings), had claimed the throne in his brother's absence.

Darius announced that this person was not truly Bardiya, but a charlatan and magician named Gaumata impersonating the king's son. According to Darius, Bardiya had been dead for quite some time: Cambyses II had quietly slain his brother before setting off for Egypt. So Darius, with the aid of six other Persian nobles, slew Bardiya and assumed the crown for himself. He defended his actions, stating that he was restoring the Achaemenid family to their rightful place on the Persian throne as a member—though distant—of the royal family. However, people did not readily accept Darius I as their monarch, and much of his time in power was spent quelling various insurrections and rebellions.

One was the Ionian Revolt, which unfolded in the early 5th century BCE. This conflict, sparked by a desire for Greek autonomy and fueled by resentment of Persian oppression, was a prelude to the larger Greco-Persian Wars and had profound ramifications for the ancient world.

At its core, the Ionian Revolt was a response to the heavy-handed rule of the Persians, who had subjected the Ionian Greeks to their authority following the conquest of Lydia by Cyrus the Great in 547 or 546 BCE. The Ionian Greeks, particularly those in city-states like Miletus and Ephesus, yearned to break free from Persian dominance and restore their traditional Greek governance. Although the Ionian Greeks were still in nominal control of their various city-states, all were answerable to the Persian *satrap*, or local governor whom the Persian monarch appointed. The Ionian desire for independence found support from politicians in Athens and Eretria, who perceived this as a golden opportunity to challenge and check Persian expansion and extend their influence in the region.

In 499 BCE, the city of Miletus, led by their tyrant, Aristagoras, ignited the rebellion by rising against Persian rule. Tasked with overseeing Miletus on behalf of the Persian Empire, Aristagoras was recently appointed to his role after his predecessor and father-in-law, Histiaeus, lost Darius' trust and was imprisoned in the Persian city of Susa in southern Iran (present-day Shush). However, Aristagoras proved to be just as problematic for the Persians as his father-in-law. His defiance quickly spread to other Ionian city-states, with the high-water mark for the Ionian rebels being the capture and burning of Sardis, the former Lydian capital and a key Persian stronghold.

The Athenians and Eretrians lent their military support to the Ionians, and together, they sought to thwart Persian control in the region and further Greek influence. In response, King Darius I of Persia launched a formidable counteroffensive, recapturing the Ionian cities, culminating in the fall of Miletus in 494 BCE. Aristagoras left Miletus for Thrace, hoping to establish a colony for the Ionian Greeks, but Thracians ultimately killed him. Histiaeus, though initially escaping Persian clutches at Susa, was caught by the *satrap* Artaphernes in Sardis and crucified. In the ensuing years, the revolt's failure led to harsher measures and increased Persian control over the

Ionian Greeks. Meanwhile, the aftermath of the revolt led to an increased distaste for Persian power among the Greeks, both in Anatolia and elsewhere.

Though the Ionian Revolt ultimately ended in a Persian victory and the reassertion of Persian authority over the region, its consequences were far-reaching. It marked the start of the Greco-Persian War. This early conflict demonstrated the Greeks' resolve and willingness to stand against Persian expansion, setting the stage for the historic battles and events that would follow.

Incensed by what he saw as the audacity of the Greeks to rise against him and angered by the aid rendered to the Ionians from Athens and Eretria, Darius moved against Greece in 492 BCE with the first Persian invasion of Greece. On the other side of the Aegean, the Greek city-states prepared for a defensive struggle that would come to define their identity. Greece, a patchwork of fiercely independent city-states, was a land where democracy took root in Athens, philosophy flourished, and the courage of Spartan warriors was legendary. They had no intention of submitting to the might of Persia.

Darius, through his nephew and son-in-law, Mardonius, had pushed Persian rule as far as Macedonia in Europe, just north of the independent Greek city-states. Emissaries were sent to the *poleis* requesting "earth and water," representing Greek capitulation to the larger Persian

Empire. Though these requests were not met, it was a clear signal to the Greek city-states that a full-scale invasion of the Persian war machine was imminent. As a result, *poleis* that had long been at loggerheads, like Athens and Sparta, quickly began to unite to deal with the greater Persian threat.

While Athens and Sparta temporarily set aside their differences, they did not collaborate on a joint military action during this period. Instead, they both acknowledged the looming threat of a Persian invasion. Given its proximity to the Persian advance, Athens faced the immediate danger of being the first major city to be conquered. The Persians began on the island of Euboea, capturing the *poleis* of Carystus and Eretria. From there, the fleet sailed toward the Greek mainland, landing on the plains of Marathon in 490 BCE. This location, 26.2 miles northeast of Athens, posed a significant threat.

Under the leadership of their general, Miltiades, the Athenians requested assistance from other Greek states. While allies from Plataea responded, the majority of the troops defending against the threat were from Athens. A detachment of approximately 10,000 *hoplites* (foot soldiers armed with spears and shields) marched to protect their homeland. Sparta, according to Herodotus, was willing to help. However, they stated that their armies could not move until the conclusion of the religious festival of Carneia—a celebration to appease Apollo that forbade Sparta to partake in warmongering. The Persian force was formidable, numbering in the tens of thousands. Archers, infantry, and cavalry formed the core of the Persian army, ready to decimate the Greeks by land, while a fleet of Persian warships awaited the conclusion of the battle offshore, primed to strike Athens by sea.

Miltiades faced a challenging decision. He knew the Persian fleet could wreak havoc on Athens while the Greek *hoplites* were engaged in battle. Time was crucial, so the Greek commanders decided that directly confronting the Persians using the *phalanx* was the best approach. A *phalanx* is a classic Greek military formation where *hoplites* stood shoulder to shoulder in rows, each holding a shield and spear. This close-knit arrangement formed a defensive shield wall, challenging the enemy to penetrate. This strategy was a key feature of Greek warfare and required teamwork and synchronization during combat.

In a daring move, the Greek *hoplites* charged across the plain of Marathon, closing the distance to the Persian lines, hoping to avoid their deadly archers. Despite being outnumbered, they formed a cohesive and resilient *phalanx*, and their bronze shields provided an unyielding wall. Thus, the Battle of Marathon erupted in a fierce clash of arms as Persian arrows and Greek spears filled the sky. The Greeks' bold maneuvers paid off, intimidating the Persian forces. The *hoplites* on the Greek wings bore down upon the Persian flanks, creating gaps in their lines. The Persian center, now weakened and wavering, was vulnerable. The Greeks, led by Miltiades, launched a decisive thrust, penetrating the heart of the Persian army. As the dust settled, it became clear that the Greeks had achieved a miraculous victory. The Persian force was routed, and the Greeks pursued their fleeing foes to the shores, capturing seven Persian ships.

The contemporary 26.2-mile footrace gets its name from the plains of Marathon. This connection stems from the story of Pheidippides (also known as Phidippides or Philippides), an ancient Greek runner. Before the Battle of Marathon, Pheidippides was sent from Athens to Sparta to request aid. The first half of the journey was a grueling 150 miles that he is said to have conquered in two days. This, too, has sparked a modern-day footrace called the Spartathalon, though it is understandably not as common as a marathon. Later, as the Battle of Marathon raged to a close, Pheidippides was dispatched to carry a message to Athens, 26.2 miles away from the battle site, to deliver the news of the Athenian victory.

It's said that Pheidippides tragically died soon after delivering his message, uttering "We're victorious," before collapsing. The first organized marathon race occurred at the Athens Olympics in 1896 CE, covering a distance close to the legend of Pheidippides' journey from Marathon to Athens. How much of Pheidippides' story is fact and how much is legend is unclear. Herodotus does mention his lengthy journey to Sparta, but not the fatal final run to Athens. The first source to discuss a messenger dying after relaying the Athenian victory is Plutarch, a Greek philosopher and historian from the 1st century CE. Interestingly, his messenger is not named Pheidippides, but Eucles (or Eukles). It is Lucian, a Greek rhetorician from the 2nd century CE, who ties the story of the messenger dying to Pheidippides.

The Battle of Marathon was a defining moment in Greek history, particularly for Athens, demonstrating the courage and resilience of the free Greek city-states against overwhelming odds. The triumph at Marathon saved Athens from immediate peril and sent a powerful message to their neighboring city-states and the world.

After the embarrassing rout at Marathon, Persia was not interested in quietly fading away. The invasion of Greece was meant to continue straight away, but the death of Darius I in 486 BCE and several uprisings, particularly one in Egypt, considerably delayed Persian forces. Thus, an entire decade passed before the shadow of Persia darkened Greece's shores once more.

The Achaemenid Empire continued under the command of Darius' son, Xerxes I (also known as Xerxes the Great or Khshayarsha). Xerxes was fond of more heavy-handed tactics than his father when suppressing rebellion and discord. Egypt was still in chaos when Xerxes ascended the throne, and despite the desire to go after the Greek city-states, he recognized that his first order of business had to be quelling the portions of his empire that were in open revolt. Consequently, he dispatched the bulk of his focus and forces to Egypt.

In 484 BCE, Xerxes swiftly subdued the Nile Delta, employing much harsher tactics than his father ever did to bring territories under Persian control. Simultaneously, Babylonia—sometimes known as Mesopotamia and nestled between the Tigris and Euphrates Rivers—was stirred into rebellion. Babylon held immense importance within the Persian Empire due to its strategic location, rich cultural heritage, and profound symbolic significance. However, Babylon grappled with intricate political and religious tensions beneath its wealth and prestige.

This undercurrent of unrest was exacerbated by religious and cultural frictions, with two particular Babylonian kings at the helm of the rebellion. Having been under Persian rule for approximately fifty years, the Babylonians' dissatisfaction with their foreign overseers had reached a boiling point. The imposition of Persian governance and cultural norms faced stiff resistance in Babylon. Moreover, the Persian administration's negligence in observing local religious and cultural rites further alienated the Babylonian populace. In his characteristic fashion, Xerxes clamped down on the revolt, imposing severe repercussions on Babylon.

Before these rebellions under the reign of Darius I, the Achaemenids had treated Egypt and Babylonia more or less like their own kingdoms despite being under the rule of a *satrap*. The Achaemenid kings would name them-selves "King of Egypt and Babylonia," recognizing the historical and cultural influence of these great kingdoms in their respective regions. However, after 484 BCE, Xerxes abandoned these titles and essentially sought to erase the nominal independence of Babylonia and Egypt, styling himself simply as the "King of the Persians and the Medes." His Empire would be called Persia—not the conglomerate of various states and kingdoms his father had commanded.

As soon as Xerxes stifled the flames in Babylon, he eagerly turned his eyes back to Greece, embarking on the most well-known campaign of his reign. Following his father's defeat at the Battle of Marathon, he was determined to realize his empire's ambitions and avenge the loss. He was likely eager to show his might as a ruler after the back-to-back repudiations of his authority in Babylonia and Egypt. This determination led to the Second Persian Inva-sion of Greece, a colossal undertaking of historic proportions.

In 480 BCE, Xerxes assembled a diverse amalgamation of troops drawn from the vast territories under Persian control. This included infantry, cavalry, and a formidable navy, all with the express goal of invading the Greek city-states. Knowing the unsettled wilderness they would likely traverse, this massive host included fierce warriors, laborers, and artisans to build bridges and roads for the Persian campaign. However, no size, prowess, or preparedness could address the challenges the army would face during their journey.

It began with a relentless overland march until they neared the Hellespont. According to Herodotus, to overcome this obstacle, engineers were sent ahead to construct two bridges made of boats across the strait. The construction was a monumental task that involved linking boats to create a stable pathway for the troops and equipment to cross. The exact details of the bridge vary in historical accounts, but it was nevertheless a remarkable achievement in logistics and engineering.

Unfortunately for the king, the first set of bridges was destroyed in a storm before the Persian army reached the Hellespont. Legend has it that Xerxes was infuriated with not only his engineers but with the water itself. All those responsible for the initial construction were beheaded, and the Persian king ordered a list of punishments for the disobedient water. These included whipping the strait three hundred times, casting manacles into the waves, and branding the water with a hot iron while soldiers shouted at it.

Ultimately, the bridge of boats was remade, and the army —taking seven days to cross it—lumbered on into Thrace. By Herodotus' count, the Persian army was five million strong. However, modern historians believe that number to be grossly inflated, estimating Xerxes' forces to be somewhere around 360,000 with anywhere between seven hundred and eight hundred ships to support them. Even though this is significantly less than five million, it remained a daunting force for the fragmented Greek city-states, who perceived the looming Persian threat as ominously as the sword of Damocles hanging above them.

Nevertheless, the slow speed of the army bought the Greeks some much-needed time to prepare their defenses. Roughly thirty Greek city-states were ready and willing to resist the Persian onslaught; this time, the *polis* of Sparta spearheaded the efforts. A congress of delegates convened, with each member state receiving one vote, though a majority would rule. They agreed to cease all hostilities between one another and chose the military giant of Sparta to command their united military defense.

Naval power was handed over to an Athenian named Themistocles, who commanded a force of triremes. A trireme was an ancient Mediterranean warship character-ized by its sleek and slender design, typically powered by three rows of oarsmen. These vessels were known for their exceptional speed and maneuverability, making them crucial in naval warfare during antiquity.

Aware of what was approaching, the Spartans decided to make their first stand against the Persian juggernaut at Thermopylae, a narrow mountain pass in central Greece with significant strategic value. It served as a natural chokepoint that controlled access from Thessaly into central Greece, making it a critical defensive position for the Greeks. King Leonidas I of Sparta, selected to lead the Greek armies, took a force of six to seven thousand *hoplites* from Sparta, Athens, Thebes, and more towards the tapering passage, hoping to head off the massive Persian force before they could sweep into the bulk of Greece.

Once at Thermopylae, a name which translates to "Hot Gates," Leonidas took up a defensive position, aware that the confined landscape disadvantaged the bulky Persian military. In August 480 BCE, Xerxes arrived with his troops in tow, and the Greeks braced for the Persian assault. For two days, Leonidas and the Greeks valiantly held the line, repelling wave after wave of Persian attacks.

While the land battle at Thermopylae raged on, simultaneously, off the coast, the Greek and Persian fleets clashed at Artemisium. Xerxes sought to advance his forces southward through central Greece, and both sides understood that controlling the seas was vital to their respective goals. Eurybiades, an experienced Spartan admiral, was waiting with 271 triremes off the northern coast of Euboea. During the initial day of the battle, Xerxes secretly dispatched 200 ships to circumnavigate the island of Euboea, aiming to block the Euripus Strait and trap the Greek navy. Later that day, Eurybiades and his fleet discovered this move and engaged the main Persian fleet, achieving modest success.

The Greeks intended to sail south in the morning to confront the Persian detachment, but weather conditions disrupted their plans. That night, a storm struck, keeping the Greek fleet trapped at Artemisium. However, this weather change fortuitously caused the 200 Persian ships, intended to block the Euripus Strait, to be scuttled. So, as the second day dawned, the Persian and Greek triremes resumed their hostilities off the coast of Euboea while the Persian infantry continued to slam into the Greek *hoplites* braced at Thermopylae.

Despite being grossly outnumbered, things were going better than expected for the Greeks. Unfortunately, this would not continue. A local Greek named Ephialtes, seeking reward from the Persians, revealed a mountain path that allowed the enemy to bypass the Greek position at Thermopylae. The Persian Immortals, an elite fighting unit, crept along the hidden trail, emerging behind the Greek position as the sun rose on the third day of battle.

Realizing defeat was imminent, Leonidas dismissed most of his troops, dispatching them south so the Greek army could live to fight another day. He retained a small detachment of *hoplites* from Sparta, Thespiae, and Thebes, including his 300-member royal guard. Despite being vastly outnumbered and encircled, these men defended Thermopylae for as long as they could, with the exception of the Theban group, who chose to surrender. Leonidas and his 300 fought down to the last man and stood as a poetic testament to the courage and sacrifice of Greek warriors, particularly the Spartans.

The Battle of Thermopylae, though a tactical defeat for the Greeks, became a symbol of resilience and determination. Leonidas' selfless heroism inspired the subsequent battles of the Greco-Persian Wars. But this influence extended beyond the Ancient Greeks; Thermopylae has left an enduring legacy in Western culture and continues to be eulogized on the stage and screen in the modern era.

With the fall of Thermopylae, the Greek navy decided to withdraw and seek a more strategic location. The waters around Euboea were too open for the Greek fleet to take on the sizeable Persian navy successfully, so the triremes sailed south for the narrow straits around the island of Salamis.

After slaughtering what remained of the Greek forces at Thermopylae, Xerxes proceeded south, targeting the prominent city of Athens. In September of 480, Persian forces captured and sacked Athens, dealing a significant emotional blow to the Greeks, particularly the Athenians. Though few Athenians remained in the city—most having evacuated to the Peloponnesian town of Troezen or the nearby islands of Aegina and Salamis—the physical infrastructure of Athens was subject to widespread destruction.

Xerxes ordered the city to be put to the torch, and much of Athens's architecture and historical treasures were lost to the flames, including the iconic temples on the Acropolis. The Old Parthenon, an older temple dedicated to the goddess Athena, was one such loss. Though it was rebuilt into a new and beautiful temple during the Classical Age, the destruction of the original was still a profound loss of cultural heritage. However, the mistreatment of their city further galvanized the Athenians and their Greek allies against the Persian invaders, highlighting the importance of defending their homeland and preserving their culture in the face of possible erasure.

Meanwhile, the Greek navy, which had fled Artemisium and hurried south, was waiting for their Persian pursuers in the Saronic Gulf off the coast of Athens. Themistocles, cognizant that once again a strategic location was needed to thwart the larger Persian fleet, coyly lured them into a narrow strait of water between the island of Salamis and the coastal town of Piraeus by feigning a retreat.

On September 28, 480 BCE, as the Persian commanders sailed their ships into the waterway, the Greeks closed in from both sides, trapping the Persian fleet. With the Persian numerical advantage handily neutralized, the confined waters of Salamis turned the battle into a chaotic and brutal contest. The smaller Greek triremes, highly maneuverable and skilled in close combat, inflicted significant damage on the Persian vessels, whose commanders struggled to coordinate their forces in the tight space.

The Greek victory at Salamis was decisive, becoming one of the first major naval battles recorded in history. Real- izing their advantage, the Greeks sank or captured a significant portion of the Persian fleet, damaging Persian naval power, thwarting Xerxes' plans, and shaking the psyche of the Persian war machine. Embarrassed, the Persian king and his fleet—still outnumbering the Greeks —turned from Salamis and limped to Asia Minor.

As a turning point in the Greco-Persian Wars, the Battle of Salamis demonstrated that Greek unity, naval skill, and strategic acumen could successfully oppose the might of the Persian Empire. Salamis showcased the importance of naval power in antiquity and underlined the significance of clever tactics in the face of seemingly insurmountable odds. It further served as a glowing symbol of Greek mili- tary intelligence and set the stage for the eventual Greek victory in the Greco-Persian Wars.

Though Xerxes himself had decamped back towards Asia Minor, a detachment of the Persian army was left on mainland Greece under the command of Mardonius, the king's cousin and brother-in-law. The troops passed the winter at Thessaly, and diplomatic discussions between Mardonius and the Greeks continued into the summer of 479 BCE. August saw the Persians ensconced in a fortified position near the city of Plataea, in the region of Boeotia south of Thessaly.

The Greek city-states had maintained their alliance, and Sparta continued to supply military leadership in the form of Pausanias, a general and current commander of the Greek forces. The expulsion of the Persians from the Greek city-states remained their paramount goal. As a result, the Greek troops were encamped close to the Persian position near Plataea, maintaining a strategic location on the high ground above the Persian camp.

Before the main battle, several skirmishes and minor clashes between the two armies highlighted the continued Persian numerical advantage and showcased the Greeks' tenacity and discipline. Finally, the main battle occurred when Mardonius initiated an attack on the Greek position. Rather than scatter in fright before the Persian onslaught, Pausanias opted to keep his army in a tightly packed *phalanx*, and the Persians were unable to break their formation. Eventually, the Greeks used their strategic location to their advantage and charged downhill, overwhelming the Persians and securing a Greek victory.

Though the battle was not as clearly won as at Salamis, Mardonius was killed, further demoralizing the Persian forces. Confusion reigned, and the remaining Persian troops retreated in disarray. The Greeks pursued them, destroying their camp as they went and finally expelling the Persians from Greece. The Greeks had successfully defended their homeland and repelled the Persian invaders, securing their independence and perhaps the very future of Western civilization.

Western historians tend to see the Greek victory as a huge turning point for the rise of Western civilization. After all, had the Persians overwhelmed the Greeks and added them to the morass of their empire, the world would likely look quite different now. The accomplishments of Classical Greece might never have come to fruition, and many roots and seeds of Western thought and culture come from the ideas generated during that time. However, one should be cautious of casting the Greeks as the ideal defenders of freedom and liberty and the Persians as dark overlords hoping to destroy all individualistic thought. History, as always, is more nuanced than that. What can be declared without hesitation is that the Greek victory certainly shaped the fate of the world.

In the end, Xerxes' campaign had not only failed to subdue Greece but also drained the Persian Empire's resources and demoralized its forces. The Second Persian Invasion of Greece marked a turning point in the Greco-Persian Wars, with the Greek city-states successfully defending their independence against the might of the Achaemenid Empire. It also marked the beginning of the Achaemenian decline—Xerxes withdrew from military campaigns, instead becoming more interested in the machinations of his court, particularly his harem. He and his eldest son were assassinated by a politician named Artabanus in 465

BCE, and his younger son, Artaxerxes I, took the Achaemenid throne. Though the empire remained in existence until its eventual destruction by Alexander the Great in 330 BCE, it continued to roil with revolts and gradually shrunk over the following century. It never again reached the heights it achieved under Cyrus, Darius, and Xerxes.

With the Persians gone, Sparta had no reason or will to continue fighting and did not wish to pursue their antagonists across the ocean to Asia. Athens, on the other hand, had a different idea. Eager to come to the aid of the Ionian Greeks once again and prepared to deploy their navy to do so, the Athenians formed the Delian League. This was a federation of primarily Greek states led by the Athenians and headquartered on the Cycladic island of Delos. The organization was similar to the alliance the Greek city-states had struck during the Greco-Persian War, with each state possessing representation and equal voting power. Most of the Aegean islands joined except for Aegina, Melos, and Thera, as did most of the city-states located on the Chalcidice peninsula, those states around the Hellespont and the Bosporus straits, and most of the Ionian *poleis.*

Established around 478 BCE, the Delian League was formed primarily to counter the threat of Persian invasion following the Greco-Persian Wars. Initially, its contributions and resources were pooled to ensure the common defense against Persia, and for the first ten years, the focus was mainly on enacting retribution against the empire. One example was the victory at the Battle of Eurymedon near Pamphylia in Asia Minor, with the Delian League prevailing over the Persian army and navy.

Over time, the democratic nature of the Delian League was lost, and Athens began to dominate. Much of the foreign policy from 461 BCE onward was driven by Athenian will, and the league's treasury was relocated from Delos to the Athenian Acropolis. Member states were expected to provide support through financial contributions or with ships and soldiers. Essentially, the Delian League morphed from a defensive alliance into a means of extending Athenian power and influence into the Aegean region. Athens' rise to power understandably created tensions and conflict within the league and contributed to the outset of hostilities between Athens and Sparta.

Regarding the Persian problem, hostilities persisted. The Athenians and their allies supported another Egyptian revolt against Persia in 460 BCE. In 454 BCE, the Persians annihilated the Greek navy after the uprisings in Egypt were once again quashed. However, from 450 to 449 BCE, the Delian League carried out a series of attacks on the Persian-held island of Cyprus. Finally, in 449 BCE, the Peace of Callias was established between Artaxerxes I of Persia and Athens and its allies. For peace to be established, the Achaemenid Empire committed to officially recognizing Greek city-states' independence in Europe and Asia Minor and promised not to enter the Aegean Sea.

With the formal conclusion of the Greco-Persian Wars, Greece was once again free to look inward. The Classical Era had begun, and with it, a fight for dominance on the Greek mainland was brewing. Athens and Sparta, with a long history of tension and rivalry, were poised to rip Greece in two as the struggle for supremacy began.

5

A STRUGGLE FOR SUPREMACY
(460–359 BCE)

I n the history of Ancient Greece, few conflicts have left as lasting an impact as the Peloponnesian Wars. A prolonged and ruinous conflict, it wasn't merely a clash of city-states but also a face-off between the core values and structures shaping the Greek world. As Athens and Sparta, two formidable powers, clashed in a monumental struggle for supremacy, a period of relentless warfare, shifting alliances, and deep-seated rivalries unfolded. This chapter explores the detailed series of events, political strategies, and confrontations that characterized the Peloponnesian War, shedding light on a dispute that transformed Ancient Greece and offered timeless insights into power dynamics, partnerships, and the human toll of warfare.

Despite the years of conflict during the Greco-Persian Wars, the Athenian government grew into its own. As discussed in Chapter III, Cleisthenes and his reforms guided the city-state ever closer to true democracy. During the Persian Wars, citizens continued participating in the assembly, where important decisions were made. Leadership positions, like that of the *strategoi* (generals), were open to citizens, though often held by members of the aristocracy. In the face of the Persian threat, Athens needed to make crucial strategic decisions. As a result, the leadership often fell to influential and well-connected individuals, such as Themistocles or Miltiades. It would have been easy to slip into an oligarchy or even a tyranny during the years of war. However, Athens managed to walk a fine line, placing strong leaders in power while still maintaining a check on their capacity for absolutism. So, despite a degree of centralization required to address Persian aggression, the Athenians attempted to retain their democratic experiment.

After driving out Persia from the Greek mainland in 480 BCE, Athens rose to prominence, strengthened by the support of the Delian League and the power it brought. This period, though it coincided with the Peloponnesian War, is often referred to as the Golden Age of Athens. It is primarily associated with the leadership of Pericles, the statesman who oversaw many of the transformative developments that characterized this era.

Born around 495 BCE, Pericles was a member of an aristocratic Athenian family and received an excellent education. He entered politics and held various key positions, including that of *strategos* (general) in the Athenian military. As a military leader, Pericles led Athens through significant conflicts in the Persian and Peloponnesian Wars. He was a leading figure in the democratic faction and a staunch advocate for Athenian democracy, expanding the role of ordinary citizens in the government and making it more inclusive. His policies increased opportunities for the lower classes to participate in public life.

Aside from his military acumen and political prowess, Pericles was also an important cultural patron, presiding over the artistic achievements of the Golden Age of Athens. The earliest date noted in Pericles' life is his financial support of Aeschylus' Persian trilogy in 472 BCE. He supported the arts, philosophy, and architecture, including the reconstruction of the Parthenon on the Acropolis.

As the Golden Age flourished, the city became a hub for artists, philosophers, and playwrights, with renowned figures like Aeschylus, Sophocles, Euripides, and Aristophanes producing some of their most celebrated works. Prominent philosophers such as Socrates, Plato, and Xenophon emerged, establishing the groundwork for Western philosophy and sparking intellectual discussions that still resonate in contemporary thought. With so many eminent figures, citizens often had access to an exceptional education. The Athenian educational system emphasized the development of well-rounded citizens, including instruction in subjects like music, physical fitness, and philosophy.

Pericles oversaw significant public works, including building the "Long Walls," which linked Athens to its port at Piraeus. This ensured the safe movement of goods and soldiers. This access to the sea reinforced Athenian dominance in the region. The city-state already had control over major trade routes thanks to its impressive navy and primary position within the Delian League.

Sparta, Athens' longstanding rival, viewed Athens' achievements with suspicion and envy. The Spartans did not want to continue aggression against the Persians after the Battle of Plataea, and as a result, they remained isolated from the Delian League. In truth, Sparta could not seem to stick to one prerogative, frequently oscillating between isolationism and imperialism. Sparta eventually decided that the expansion of Athens was no longer tolerable, so they took up a leadership role with their own Peloponnesian League, aiming to counterbalance the power and influence of the Delian League.

Primarily composed of city-states in the Peloponnese, notable members included Corinth, Megara, and Thebes. The coalition predated the Delian League, founded well before the outbreak of the Peloponnesian War, back when Sparta was more concerned with the internal threats of its *helots* than with external aggressors. Membership fluctuated over the years, but it was the oldest and most enduring political association in Ancient Greece.

Unlike the Delian League, there was no overarching agreement binding the states together; members made their own arrangements with Sparta. In further contrast with the Delian League, the Peloponnesian League did not ask for any tribute. It only required its members to supply military aid when called upon during war. Galled by the Athenians' ever-growing influence, the Peloponnesian League began to martial their forces.

It should be noted that there were technically two Peloponnesian Wars. The first is frequently overshadowed by the magnitude of the Persian War and the more famous second Peloponnesian War. Also referred to as the Great Peloponnesian War, it was from 460 to 445 BCE, and though Sparta was involved, it largely began as a conflict between Athens and Corinth, with Sparta supporting Corinth.

So, what exactly was Athens up to that enraged the member states of the Peloponnesian League? During the immediate aftermath of Salamis, Plataea, and the Persian retreat, relations between the Greek city-states were strained but polite. Sparta was wary of Athenian ambition, and rightly so, as the Delian League's dynamics shifted and Athens became increasingly aggressive. Sparta was not alone in its skepticism of Athenian motivations, and after Athens allied itself with Argos and Megara—two city-states very near the isthmus of Corinth—the Corinthians and other *poleis* on the Peloponnese felt quite threatened. Furthermore, the Athenian subjugation of Aegina, a historical stronghold of Doric culture, outraged both the Spartans and other Peloponnesians.

The fights between Corinth, Athens, Sparta, and their other various allies were evenly matched, and there was no straightforward winner. Thus, fifteen years of skirmishing over geographical, political, and religious differences ensued. The Athenians were war-weary since the First Peloponnesian War, and they also had friction in Boeotia to the north and Euboea to the east that diverted their attention. Furthermore, there is not as much space dedicated to the conflict in the pages of history as the earlier Persian War and the later Peloponnesian War. So, it is difficult to parse out the particularities of the conflict.

Nevertheless, the Peloponnesian and Attic parties resolved to settle the matter with the Thirty Years' Peace. Though there was no clear winner, this established a balance of power in Greece, essentially dividing it into a sphere of Athenian influence and a separate sphere of Spartan control. However, it was a bit of a blow to Athens' expansionary ambitions and defensive planning. The loss of Megara, a strategically important city located at the entrance of the Corinthian isthmus, meant that Athens was far more vulnerable to Spartan aggression in the future.

Yet the balance of power was fragile, with both sides distrustful of the other. The tension between Athens and Sparta wasn't resolved; it merely lay dormant after the Thirty Years' Peace was established. Regardless, Athens, under Pericles, continued to work on expanding their influence, working eastward this time. In the 430s BCE, he led an expedition to the Black Sea, hoping to expand Athenian power by forging close ties with city-states in the region, particularly those in and around the Bosporus.

Around the same time, the Athenians also established the colony of Amphipolis near the Chalcidice peninsula. This was not far from the Corinthian colony of Potidaea, and the proximity, coupled with the Athenians' new alliance with Arcarnania, a traditionally Corinthian-influenced region, inflamed Corinth's temper once again. They soon went even further, with Athens asking Potidaea for financial tribute while simultaneously economically pressuring Megara through an embargo.

These actions sent other city-states into the arms of Sparta, begging for its protection, but Sparta continued to keep its counsel, upholding the terms of the Thirty Years' Peace. The situation worsened, however, when a disagreement between Corinth and its colony of Corcyra ballooned into a bigger conflict. Athens stood on the side of Corcyra while the Peloponnesian League backed Corinth. At this point, Sparta believed Athens to be in direct violation of the Thirty Years' Peace Treaty and indicated that this could lead to war. Pericles, unwilling to back down, held the Athenians' ground. When shaky attempts at diplomacy failed between Sparta and Athens, it seemed that all-out war was the only solution.

So, in the spring of 431 BCE, Spartan-allied Thebes struck the Athenian ally of Plataea, and the Peloponnesian War was underway. The first half of the conflict, sometimes called the Archidamian War in honor of the Spartan king Archidamus II, unfolded from 431 to 421 BCE. The Spartans invaded Athenian lands every year, aiming to trigger a significant confrontation. However, the Athenians employed a strategy of retreating behind the Long Walls, which protected the city of Athens and allowed them to maintain their sea access through the port of Piraeus. Pericles wisely used Athenian naval supremacy, choosing instead to menace the Peloponnesian allies' coasts and shipping routes.

Crouching behind tall walls in confined spaces can lead to issues such as the spread of disease. During the second year of the war, a brutal plague swept through Athens, decimating the populace and claiming the lives of many high-ranking civilians, including Pericles himself. Despite being ravaged in both mind and body by illness, the Athenians managed to hold the Spartans at bay during the plague years, with neither side making significant gains.

After the epidemic subsided, Athens regained its momentum. The Athenians boldly attacked Syracuse on the island of Sicily and launched military expeditions into the

Peloponnesian peninsula. But their successes were short-lived. Sparta countered with a significant victory at Amphipolis, where the Athenian leader, Cleon, was defeated. Following this setback, the Athenian general Nicias negotiated a tenuous peace.

The Peace of Nicias was hardly ironclad, and each side spent the ensuing six years trying to outmaneuver the other through diplomatic skullduggery and small-scale military operations. It was fragile and did little to address the underlying issues that precipitated the war in the first place. It is easier to think of the short-lived Peace of Nicias as a small détente or cease-fire.

The illusion of tranquility was shattered in 415 BCE when Athens launched another campaign in Sicily. The second half of the war, also known as the Decelean or Ionian War, was marked by significant shifts in power and the escalation of hostilities. From 415 to 413 BCE, Athens, under the leadership of Alcibiades, advanced on Sicily, hoping to conquer the western Greek city-states. Also known as the "Sicilian Disaster," the Sicilian Expedition was a failure for Athens. Their forces were defeated by a combined force of Syracusans and Spartans, and many Athenian ships and soldiers were lost, with destruction raining down on them even as they retreated.

Internally, Athens struggled. The defeat demoralized the populace; the war deeply affected everyone, and the fragile democratic system broke under the strain. In a coup in 411 BCE, a council of virulently anti-democratic oligarchs, known as the Council of the Four Hundred, seized power. They were soon replaced by a more moderate oligarchy, the Five Thousand. Democracy was restored quickly, returning to Athens by 410 BCE, but the political unrest continued.

Despite their victory in Sicily, Sparta was aware that they still didn't have the same financial might as Athens. They hoped to find a powerful ally who could provide funding and naval support for the Peloponnesian League. Oddly enough, it was their old adversaries, the Persian Empire, whom they decided to court. Whatever grudge Sparta may have held against the Achaemenids was nothing that gold could not heal—after all, "the enemy of my enemy is my friend."

The financial support of the Persians allowed Sparta to at last build a respectable fleet, and under the command of Lysander, the Peloponnesian navy managed to deal the Athenians a series of naval defeats, loosening their long-held grip of the seas. The Athenian navy suffered a devastating loss at the Battle of Aegospotami in 405 BCE. Following this, Spartan forces blockaded Athens and effectively quelled their resistance. Starving and weakened, the Golden Age of Athens came to a tragic end as it succumbed to Sparta, marking the conclusion of the Athenian Empire. The Long Walls of Pericles were destroyed, the Athenian navy was reduced to twelve ships, and the democratic government fell.

Now, roiled by economic difficulties and internal strife, a pro-Spartan oligarchic government known as the Thirty Tyrants ruled harshly over Athens for the following year. Under the leadership of Critias and Theramenes, the Thirty Tyrants imposed a punitive rule characterized by purges, political clampdowns, and the killing of perceived enemies. Their policies aimed to consolidate power and eradicate democratic opposition.

With the elimination of Athenian supremacy, Sparta became the paramount power in Ancient Greece, ushering in a period of Spartan hegemony. With the guidance of influential figures such as Lysander, Sparta's leadership extended its reach over and beyond the Peloponnesian League.

Yet their rule in Athens was short-lived, as internal divisions and external pressures, including resistance from democratic exiles and other Greek states, ultimately led to their downfall. In 403 BCE, the democratic general Thrasybulus led a successful revolt, restoring Athens' democratic institutions and ending this dark chapter in the city's history. He and his forces began at the fortress at Phyle, which served as their strategic base. From there, Thrasybulus and his democratic supporters engaged the forces of the Thirty Tyrants in the decisive battle of Munychia near the port of Piraeus. Thrasybulus was victorious, with this battle being a significant turning point in the struggle to restore democracy.

With the oppressive rule of the Thirty Tyrants over-thrown, the democratic institutions of Athens were restored, including the *ekklesia* and the council. Most importantly, following the victory, Thrasybulus offered an amnesty. This general pardon allowed many individuals, even some who had supported the Thirty Tyrants, to return to Athens without facing repercussions. Though never quite as dominant as before, Athens slowly rebuilt. General Conon saw the Long Walls rebuilt, and the navy slowly gathered its strength once more, aided financially by the Persians.

The restoration of democracy in Athens was a triumph for democracy and a testament to the resilience of Athenian political traditions. Yet, the rule of the Thirty Tyrants stands as a stark reminder of the fragility of democratic values in times of conflict.

Unfortunately, the period of peace was short-lived. The decline of Athens and the ascent of Sparta under King Agesilaus II created a power imbalance that negatively impacted many other Greek city-states. A coalition was formed to challenge the new Spartan hegemony, including the *poleis* of Athens, Corinth, Argos, and Thebes. Much like Athens faced disdain for its imperial ambitions, Sparta too was now looked upon with disapproval for its own imperial aspirations. Additionally, the Achaemenid Empire was none too pleased with recent Spartan activities in Asia Minor—the current king, Artaxerxes II, had just suppressed an attempted coup led by his brother,

Cyrus, and backed by the Spartans. As a result, the Persians entered the conflict on the side of Athens.

The Corinthian War followed from 395 to 387 BCE, named for the region where most of the skirmishing occurred. Early on, most land battles were exercises in frustration, with neither Athens and its allies nor Sparta gaining the upper hand. However, fortune favored the Athenians at sea during the Battle of Cnidus in 394 BCE. In the waters off the coast of southern Anatolia, the Athenian general Conon and his Persian allies, led by Pharnabazus, decimated the Spartan navy with a decisive victory. With its ships limping back toward their harbors on the Peloponnese and another *helot* revolt underway, it seemed that the conflict would soon be over. In 392 BCE, Sparta proposed peace terms. However, Artaxerxes, still resentful of Agesilaus' support for his brother and rival to the throne, wasn't finished with Sparta. Athens was primed for battle and in no mood to cease fighting.

If Persia and Athens had remained allies, perhaps the war would have ended sooner, with much graver consequences for Sparta. However, the Athenians irritated their Persian allies through continued interference in Asia Minor. Persia was also beset again by uprisings in Egypt and Cyprus and eager to end the conflict. Realizing that supporting the Spartans would likely tamp down Athens' expansionary agenda in Anatolia, Persia turned on Athens, reuniting again with Sparta. Led by Antalcidas and aided by Persians and Syracusans, the Spartans blockaded the Hellespont against the Athenians. In a similar ending to the Peloponnesian War, Athens was starved into submission and accepted the Peace of Antalcidas, the King's Peace, in 386 BCE.

This peace agreement, guaranteed by Artaxerxes II of Persia, stated that Asia Minor, including the island of Cyprus, was to remain under Persian influence. Beyond that, all other Greek city-states were to be autonomous, except for Athens' long-held colonies of Lemnos, Imbros, and Scyros. Being on the side of the victors, Sparta's position among the Greek city-states was strengthened, while other territories saw a loss of control and a waning of influence. For instance, Thebes was forced to relinquish control of Boeotia, and a merger between the Spartan enemies of Argos and Corinth was annulled.

Although the King's Peace appeared to champion democratic principles, Sparta, being the dominant power in the region, took a flexible approach to the definition of "autonomous." As a result, Spartan dominance over Greece continued after the conclusion of the Corinthian War. They asserted themselves outside of their own territory time and time again, with a notably egregious example being the occupation of the Theban Acropolis around 382 BCE.

Spartan influence was not uncontested. One challenge came from their old adversaries: Athens formed the Second Athenian Confederacy in 378 BCE. This was similar to the old Delian League but not as imperialistic, requiring less from its member states. It mainly existed to combat Spartan aspirations on the Greek peninsulas and islands. A more intimidating challenge was the rise of Thebes, led by the brilliant tactician Epaminondas. Theban growth would later prove a formidable problem for Athens and Sparta.

After throwing the Spartans out of Thebes, the city-state steadily worked to regain influence and power over its native region of Boeotia. Furthermore, the driving source of Spartan success over the years, its military machine, finally met its match in the Theban forces commanded by Epaminondas. Alongside innovative strategies that challenged the traditional *hoplite* warfare waged by the Spartans, the Thebans also had the Sacred Band, an elite contingent of three hundred men. The Sacred Band was somewhat unique—each man was romantically paired with another, with the entire unit comprising one hundred and fifty couples. While such organizations might have been common in Ancient Greece, the Sacred Band is the most renowned among them.

Eventually, this led to the Spartan defeat on the fields of Leuctra in 371 BCE and ended King Agesilaus' supremacy over Greece. Epaminondas invaded the Peloponnese and released Messenia from centuries of Spartan bondage. These two events, coupled with Theban support for other local Peloponnesian powers like the region of Arcadia, completely undid Spartan authority on the peninsula and throughout Greece. By the 360s BCE, Sparta was no longer considered a consequential power, and Thebes continued to rise in stature, worrying the Athenians.

The next decade saw Athens and Thebes scrabbling for dominance in the wake of Sparta's fall. However, by 359 BCE, neither party had made any headway. With no major player in control of the Peloponnese and the major city-states of Boeotia and Attica arguing amongst themselves, Greece was at the mercy of a gaping power vacuum.

6

GREEK CULTURE IN THE CLASSICAL AND HELLENISTIC AGES (479–323 BCE)

Amidst the tumult and intrigue of the Greco-Persian Wars, Peloponnesian Wars, Corinthian War, and other political maneuverings of the 5th century BCE, Greek culture flourished. The renowned Classical Age birthed many of Ancient Greece's most iconic and foundational contributions in art, culture, literature, and philosophy. A significant portion of this enduring legacy originated from Athens during its illustrious Golden Age.

The ensuing chapter explores the cultural accomplishments and contributions of Ancient Greece during the Classical Age and early Hellenistic Age. These have been touched on in Chapters IV and V but merit further exploration.

Often, one of the first visual images modern humanity has of Ancient Greece, particularly of the Classical Age, is the sculpture and architecture of its temples. No matter the particular style and embellishments, an enduring sense of beauty, symmetry, and balance has trickled into Western art and architecture. A simple glance at the American capital city of Washington D.C. shows the profound impact that Classical architecture had on the Western artistic consciousness.

Classical architecture can be categorized into three distinct orders, each defined by its unique characteristics. Two of them, the Doric and Ionic orders, were developed before the Classical Age and can be seen on temples from the Archaic Era, but the third, the Corinthian order, is a product of Classical Greece.

The Doric order is the oldest and simplest of the three Greek architectural orders. It is characterized by sturdy, fluted columns with no base, rising directly from the stylobate (platform) of the temple. The columns have a plain, circular capital (top) and are topped by a square abacus, which supports the entablature. The entablature, or horizontal lintel, consists of three parts: the architrave, which is a plain, horizontal beam; the frieze, often adorned with triglyphs, or decorative grooves, and metopes, or rectangular relief panels; and the cornice, which often projects beyond the entablature. Doric temples are known for their harmonious and robust appearance and are typically seen as somewhat simple and heavy but aesthetically rewarding to behold. The Parthenon[6], in Athens, best exemplifies the style.

The Ionic order came from the Ionia region on Anatolia's western coast. It is visually more ornate and slender than the Doric, with delicately fluted columns on a smooth, rounded base. The capitals of Ionic columns are characterized by volutes, which are easily recognizable spiraled scroll-like ornaments. The entablature of the Ionic order typically features a continuous frieze adorned with intricate sculptural elements, such as figures and narrative scenes. The architrave, situated just below the ornate frieze, is often divided into three horizontal bands. The Roman historian Vitruvius once compared the Ionic order to the female shape, contrasting it with what he saw as the heavier, masculine stature of the Doric order.

The Temple of Artemis at Ephesus[7], also called the Artemesium, is a renowned example of Ionic architecture. Built by King Croesus of Lydia, it was one of the Seven Wonders of the Ancient World, though it mostly lies in ruins today. Another example, built during the Golden Age of Athens, is the Temple to Athena Nike[8] on the southwestern edge of the Athenian Acropolis.

The Corinthian order is the most elaborate of the three Greek orders, building on the Ionic order with slender, fluted columns that rest on a base. The most distinctive feature of the Corinthian columns is their ornate capitals adorned with acanthus leaves, small volutes, and other decorative elements. The entablature of the Corinthian order is similar to the Ionic, with an intricately designed frieze and cornice. The Corinthian order is less common in Greek architecture but became popular in the Hellenistic and Roman Periods. One of the most famous Greek examples is the Temple of Olympian Zeus[9] in Athens.

Outside of regal temple architecture, examples of Greek buildings in the Classical Age included the stoa and theaters. Stoa buildings were characterized by long colonnades and simple designs and served various functions, from marketplaces to places of philosophical discussion. The Stoa of Attalos[10], on the eastern side of the Athenian Agora, is an example of this kind of building, though it was built long after the height of the Classical Age. Open-air theaters were also quite popular, where plays by Aeschylus, Sophocles, and Euripides were performed. Cleverly designed to optimize acoustic properties for the audience, sites like the Theatre of Dionysus[11] in Athens stand as a testament to Athenian architectural innovation.

Many architectural features and characteristics were retained as the Classical Era transitioned into the Hellenistic Period. The Doric, Ionic, and Corinthian orders were all still used in abundance, and the emphasis on grace, beauty, balance, and symmetry continued. However, in response to the giant empire of Alexander the Great, the scope of Hellenistic architecture also widened, moving beyond the Greek world and incorporating elements from the regions he conquered. It became common to see a fusion of styles and larger forms of buildings that had been popular during the Classical Age.

For example, theaters and amphitheaters were much larger during the Hellenistic Period. Cities also became more planned, operating on a grid-like structure designed to accommodate the bustling commercial and social activities of city life.

There was often sculpture within the architecture on the outside and inside of various structures. For the Classical Greeks, sculpture aimed to create idealized, naturalistic representations of the human form. Physical beauty was heavily emphasized, and sculptors introduced the concept of *contrapposto*. In this naturalistic stance, the body's weight is unevenly distributed, leading to a more lifelike and graceful appearance. The addition of *contrapposto* elevated Greek sculpture from the blocky, stiff work of the Archaic Age into startlingly realistic work. The *Doryphoros*[12] by Polykleitos is an example of Classical *contrapposto*.

One of the most prominent sculptors of the era was the Athenian Phidias. He crafted the colossal statue of *Zeus at Olympia*[13], one of the Seven Wonders of the Ancient World, and the famous *Athena Parthenos*[14] statue that stood within the Parthenon. Sadly, neither of these impressive works has survived into modernity. There are approximations and guesses as to what they may have looked like, including a full-size replica of the *Athena Parthenos* statue in Nashville, Tennessee, USA, created by the artist Alan LeQuire.

Classical Greek architecture and sculpture demonstrated a harmonious blend of aesthetics, mathematics, and celebration of the human form. While Hellenistic sculpture did not abandon this altogether, it did embrace a more realistic and emotionally expressive style. Sculptors aimed to capture the diversity of human emotion and experience rather than just one idealized facet. Prime examples are the *Nike of Samothrace*[15], celebrated for its dynamic composition and sense of movement, *Laocoön and His Sons*[16], and *The Old Market Woman*[17].

More than just the stonework of the Greeks has survived into the present day. Much of the literature, particularly the dramas of the Classical and Hellenistic Ages, continues to be widely read and celebrated. At the time, drama in the Classical Age of Greece was a vibrant and integral part of cultural and civic life. It is divided into two primary genres: tragedy and comedy, each with distinct characteristics and themes.

The realm of tragedy often featured mythical and historical narratives, with a focus on the tragic flaws of the characters and their inevitable downfall. Questions of fate, free will, and the relationship between individuals and the gods were central. Each tragedy included a chorus, a group of performers who provided commentary on the events and themes of the play, serving as both participants and observers of the unfolding drama. These were frequently performed during citywide festivals, like the Dionysia in Athens, which provided occasions for the entire community to gather and witness theatrical productions. Outdoor theaters with stone seating were the typical venue for such events.

The three most prominent tragedians of the Classical Age were Aeschylus, Sophocles, and Euripides. Their works adhered to the classic structure of tragedy, delving into intricate moral challenges and the repercussions of human decisions. These men penned the most famous works from the time, and much of it has made it into modern educational and literary circles. Examples include Aeschylus' *Orestia*, Sophocles' *Oedipus Rex* and *Antigone*, and Euripides' *Medea* and *The Bacchae*.

On the other side was comedy. Like tragedy, it also featured a chorus. However, comedic choruses usually engaged in humorous or even bawdy and irreverent songs and dances. Comedic plots often utilized absurd and farcical elements to address contemporary issues, lampoon politicians and philosophers, and critique societal norms. Aristophanes was the most renowned comic playwright, embracing satire and wordplay to best frame his political and social commentary. *Lysistrata, The Clouds,* and *The Birds* are all well-preserved examples of his comedies.

As Greece moved into the Hellenistic Age, drama retained some elements from the earlier Classical Period but displayed distinct development in style and content. While the Hellenistic Period is often associated with the flourishing of other arts like sculpture and architecture, dramatic productions also continued to be a significant cultural and artistic expression.

Tragedy and comedy continued as prominent entertainment forms, but Hellenistic plays often featured romantic plots and themes that explored love and personal relationships. The influence of new philosophical schools like Stoicism and Epicureanism could also be detected in the drama of the period, shaping the messages around concerns of personal ethics and happiness. A shorter form of comical play known as a "mime" also gained popularity at this time, serving as a precursor to later forms of comedy. The Hellenistic Period is also considered a transitional phase in the history of drama as it eventually paved the way for the Roman theater. Greek drama greatly influenced Roman theater; Roman playwrights drew from Greek models to create their own dramatic works.

While the Hellenistic Period did not produce as many iconic playwrights as the Classical Era, it introduced new themes and genres that expanded the scope of Greek drama. These developments in Hellenistic theater contributed to the evolution of performing art in the ancient world and set the stage for the later theatrical traditions of the Roman Empire.

Outside of theatrical writing, there were various other literary accomplishments throughout the Classical Age of

Ancient Greece. There was, of course, the noble tradition of epic and lyric poetry, which was present during the Archaic times in the works of Homer and Sappho, respectively. Pindar carried on this proud poetic tradition, becoming renowned for his choral odes that celebrated the victors of the various Panhellenic Games in Ancient Greece. He often wove together elements of mythology and religion while honoring the achievements of various athletes.

In nonfiction, Herodotus, the "Father of History," wrote *The Histories*, an account of the Greco-Persian Wars and an observation of various cultures. He intermingled historical accounts with personal thought and detailed ethnographic descriptions. Thucydides' *History of the Peloponnesian War* is also considered a classic in the field of historiography, approaching history with a more analytical and objective eye that zeroed in on the causes and effects of events.

Much as the architecture of Hellenistic Greece was infused with the influence of new and previously unfamiliar cultures, so too was the literature. Hellenistic literature saw the emergence of new literary forms, including bucolic poetry, didactic poetry, and epigrams. These often rhapsodized on love, rural life, and philosophy. Theocritus, often regarded as the "Father of Bucolic Poetry," is famous for his pastoral poems set in the countryside, celebrating the beauty of nature and depicting the idyllic lives of shepherds and nymphs.

However, the tried-and-true forms of epic and lyric poetry remained as well. Though known for his small, elegant poems and epigrams, Callimachus exemplified this in his collections like *Aetia* and *Hymns*, which focused on Greek mythology and religious practices. Apollonius of Rhodes combined elements of the traditional epic with Hellenistic sensibilities. He wrote the *Argonautica*, which narrates the adventures of Jason and the Argonauts in their quest for the Golden Fleece.

As with other previously explored art forms, Hellenistic literature shifted toward more personal and intimate expressions of human experience. It explored themes of individualism, emotions, and the complexities of life, and was the direct result of the intermingling of various cultures.

Philosophy, which can be seen as another literary genre, underwent a transformative period in the Classical Era of Greece. During this time, philosophy became a distinct discipline, and key philosophical ideas and schools of thought emerged, laying the foundation for Western philosophy. In brief, philosophers, often called *sophists*, began to seek rational and systematic explanations for the nature of reality, ethics, and the cosmos.

The era began with the pre-Socratic philosophers who explored fundamental questions about the nature of the universe and the elements that compose it. Important figures emerged in Ionia, including men like Thales,

Anaximander, and Heraclitus. No one, however, looms quite as large as Socrates. He completely redefined the field and those who came after him. Known for his Socratic method of questioning, he aimed to stimulate critical thinking and self-examination with ideas centered on ethics, virtue, and the pursuit of knowledge.

His student, Plato, founded the Academy in Athens, one of the earliest known institutions of higher learning. Plato's philosophical writings often took the form of dialogues and explored an even wider range of topics than his mentor, including ethics, politics, metaphysics, and epistemology. His most famous work, *The Republic*, has shaped Western governments and societies. Plato's student, Aristotle, later established his school known as the Lyceum and significantly contributed to virtually every area of philosophy. His seminal work, *Politics*, shaped Western ideas about justice, governance, and the ideal state.

The philosophy that virtually poured out of Ancient Greece laid the groundwork for many enduring questions and ideas that continue to shape Western philosophy and intellectual inquiry. Men like Socrates, Plato, and Aristotle formed the cornerstone of Western philosophical thought, ethics, and critical thinking to this day.

The Greeks were also mathematically and scientifically inclined. During the Classical Age, significant advancements in geometry were made, especially through the contributions of Pythagoras. Famous for the Pythagorean

Theorem, Pythagoras introduced a foundational concept in geometry widely used in areas like trigonometry and engineering.

During the Hellenistic Age, advancements persisted with notable figures such as Euclid, Archimedes, and Apollonius of Perga adding to the body of knowledge. Euclid's *Elements* laid the groundwork for geometric studies for many years, introducing pivotal definitions, axioms, and theorems. Archimedes' work on calculating areas and volumes, including the method of exhaustion, was a precursor to integral calculus and supported advances in engineering. He also calculated an accurate approximation of pi and developed mechanical devices like the Archimedes screw, a simple machine used to raise water. Apollonius of Perga contributed substantially to the study of conic sections, including circles, ellipses, parabolas, and hyperbolas. His work was crucial in the development of the geometry of curves.

While we categorize these disciplines distinctly for contemporary readers, the Ancient Greeks did not differentiate between these fields as clearly as we do today. A notable philosopher might also have had his hands in mathematics, science, or medicine. Philosophers like Thales and Anaximander sought to explain the natural world through rational and systematic inquiry, laying the foundations for what is referred to as "science" today. Though remembered chiefly for his philosophical musings, Aristotle was also an important biologist. His

History of Animals served as a reference for naturalists throughout the centuries.

Although we often view medicine as a predominantly modern discipline, given the significant advancements in recent centuries, it is actually a Greek from the Classical Age who is hailed as the "Father of Medicine." Hippocrates developed a systematic approach to diagnosing and treating diseases, and the Hippocratic Oath, which emphasizes medical ethics, remains a cornerstone of the medical profession in the 21st century.

Science continued to blaze onward in the Hellenistic Age, witnessing remarkable advancements built upon the earlier Classical Period. Ideas often thought of as Renaissance-era breakthroughs were first seen at this time. Aristarchus of Samos, a Greek astronomer who lived in the 3rd century BCE, first proposed a heliocentric solar system model. This is the idea that the Earth and other planets orbit the sun. Though this was not widely accepted at the time, he was, as is now known, quite right.

One of the first maps of the known world was created during this period when Eratosthenes, a Greek mathematician from Cyrene, accurately calculated the Earth's circumference. The innovations did not stop there. Technology and engineering leaped forward with various advances in water management, mechanics, and architecture, shaping new machines and tools that aided human endeavors. One such inventor was Heron of Alexandria, a mathematician and engineer who created an early steam engine known as the *aeolipile*. His work bridged the gap between theoretical mathematics and practical engineering.

Though much of the innovation came from Athens during the Classical Era, the widening scope of intellectualism throughout the Hellenistic Period is worth noting. It is not Athens alone that is remembered as a juggernaut of intelligence and discovery, but rather all of Ancient Greece. The threads of Western cultural thought were forged here, ready to be further woven during the Roman Empire.

7

AN EMPIRE OF ONE MAN: THE TWILIGHT OF ANCIENT GREECE (359–323 BCE)

After the fall of Athens and Sparta, there was no major powerbroker in the southern portion of the Greek peninsulas—the region that has, until now, been the main focus of this text. However, in 359 BCE, a man ascended a throne to the north, and he, together with his son, brought his kingdom to the forefront of history.

Until this point, Macedon (or Macedonia) was a more sparsely inhabited, obscure region north of the Attic and Peloponnesian peninsulas. Inhabited by Greek-speaking people, they were considered culturally distinct from the southern Greek city-states and often viewed as less advanced. There are few consequential records of Macedonian history and exploits until it became clear that their fate and the fate of the southern Greek city-states were intertwined. So, the historical record regarding the predecessors of Philip II of Macedon is woefully thin.

Born in 382 BCE, Philip, often overshadowed by his son, Alexander, was a pivotal and remarkable historical figure. As the son of the former king of Macedon, Amyntas III, Philip had a front-row seat to the political storms of his native land. The kingdom seemed to be falling apart during his childhood, while his two brothers, Alexander II and Perdiccas III, tried unsuccessfully to govern and unite Macedon against outside threats. As a young man, Philip was a hostage in the city-state of Thebes during the Theban ascendancy. The Theban army, then considered the best in Greece, was under the command of the brilliant tactician Epaminondas, and Philip likely absorbed lessons from this man, either directly or indirectly.

When he came home to Macedonia, he was initially placed in a position of military command. Still, Philip found himself on the throne when his brother, Perdiccas, was unexpectedly slain while rebuffing an Illyrian invasion. Foreign threats beset the new king: the Illyrians were hovering on Macedon's western border and the Paeonians were menacing the kingdom from the north. Realizing that his army was unprepared to address the multi-faceted threats, Philip paid Illyria and Paeonia off while ceding Amphipolis back to Athens to appease their neighbors to the south. This bought him some much-needed time, and he used it wisely. Philip set about training his troops and instructing his military leaders in tactics. The *sarissa*, a large pike about one and a half times longer than the typical Greek spear, was also employed around this time.

Now confident in his forces' abilities, Philip turned his eyes to the borders of Macedon and began a campaign of expansion. In 358 BCE, he took on the Illyrians and the Paeonians and won. The following year, his marriage to Olympias, a princess from Epirus, helped to solidify the safety of Macedon's western border. He invaded Amphipolis, retaking it from the Athenians, who tried and failed for ten years to recapture their lost colony.

Once ensconced at Amphipolis, Philip began to make several forays into the heart of Thrace, a region inhabited by various independent tribes. Full of natural resources like timber, Thrace was also strategically important, opening a gateway into Asia Minor for the Macedonians. Philip also ventured southward, moving into Thessaly at a rate that disquieted the Athenians. In a moment of déjà vu, Athenian troops set up their forces at Thermopylae, hoping to block any further Macedonian expansion to the south. However, unlike Xerxes, Philip was content to wait. Refusing to engage militarily at Thermopylae, he instead acquired it via negotiation after six years.

Philip was canny, and though his army was impressive and he might have been able to overrun all of Greece and subjugate it by force, this was not his plan for the future. Rather than continue to subdue the peninsulas militarily, Philip began a protracted diplomatic campaign, hoping to bring Athens into the Macedonian fold by winning friends and influencing people. However, Athens was not so easily swayed, and figures like the great statesman and orator, Demosthenes, frequently spoke out with elegance and vigor against Philip and his Macedonian expansion.

So, between 343 and 342 BCE, when Philip was not making the headway he desired, he resumed more direct military action, bringing most of northern Greece and Thrace under his direct control. Further threatened by this display of aggression, Athens declared war in 340 BCE. In response, Philip swept south into Thessaly and Boeotia, hoping to strengthen a shaky alliance with Thebes and move on to Athens. Thebes had a different idea and decided instead to listen to Demosthenes, standing before Philip and his armies as enemies rather than friends.

At the Battle of Chaeronea in November of 339 BCE, Philip won through his skill as a general, making excellent use of his cavalry. This ended the war, and Thebes was forced to tolerate a Macedonian garrison and had its government replaced by a pro-Macedonian puppet state. As for Athens, Philip was far gentler. He still wanted a willing ally and friend in the Athenians and deeply valued their impressive navy. His ultimate goal was to march on Persia, and there was no way he could accomplish this without the Athenian navy on the seas. He allowed Athens to maintain their government, navy, and famously protective Long Walls to Piraeus, hoping to win their affection.

It was not just Athens whose cooperation he ultimately wanted against the Persians, but all of Greece. So, after the victory at Chaeronea, Philip badly desired to unite the Greeks with each other and himself. So, rather than force himself on the Greeks as their king, he formed the League of Corinth, also called the Hellenic League. It brought together a diverse assembly of Greek city-states, including former foes like Athens and Thebes, though Sparta was noticeably absent. The league's mission was twofold: to maintain a unified defense against external threats and end the incessant conflicts that had plagued the region.

In 337 BCE, Philip established a council of representatives (*synedrion*) from all the Greek states, except Sparta, with himself in the position of president (*hēgēmon*) of the league. Members were all expected to provide troops at the *hēgēmon*'s demand, and a plan was put in place to invade Asia Minor and march on Persia during the first half of 336 BCE. However, this was not to be. During a feast to celebrate the wedding of his daughter Cleopatra to his brother-in-law, Alexander of Epirus, Philip was assassinated by Pausanias, a Macedonian noble. At the time, it was believed that Pausanias had a personal quarrel with Philip, and he was killed almost immediately after murdering the king. However, over time, speculation drifted to his ex-wife, Olympias, and their son, Alexander, the two individuals with the most to gain from Philip's untimely demise. This was never substantiated, and respectable figures from the time deeply repudiated the rumor, including Aristotle, who spent a fair amount of time at Philip's court.

So passed the illustrious and wily Philip, with an unexpected and brutal death that seated his twenty-year-old son Alexander on the Macedonian throne. Though likely highly surprised at this turn of events, Alexander was, by all accounts, uncontested by his people. Upon his accession, Alexander quickly executed any potential rivals or opposition. Those who might have spoken against him probably never had the opportunity to voice their opinions.

Born in 356 BCE in the Macedonian capital of Pella to King Philip II and Queen Olympias, Alexander was tutored by the renowned philosopher Aristotle as a teenager. At a young age, he proved himself a military commander, fighting in the Battle of Chaeronea and defeating the famed and talented Sacred Band of Thebes. His position as heir was not always secure, especially once his father and mother divorced, though he and his father were reconciled before the king's death.

Ambitious, headstrong, and ruthless, Alexander was prepared to pick up Macedonian military action exactly where his father had left it, and the young king began his rule with a bang. He immediately marched south into Thessaly, ensuring that his father's conquests remained loyal. He presented himself before the League of Corinth, where he was proclaimed the new leader for the impending invasion of the Persian Empire.

However, before the expedition into Asia could be launched, Alexander had to deal with unrest in his empire. In spring 335 BCE, Alexander quelled several local invasions and rebellions. Among these, he notably destroyed Thebes when the city defied him and refused to capitulate. The city was brought to its knees, with Alexander only sparing temples and the house of the poet Pindar from his wrath. Roughly six thousand people lost their lives, and the Macedonians sold any survivors into slavery. Frightened by this display of callous destruction, the remainder of the Greek city-states quickly fell in line behind Alexander, but just to be sure, he left behind Macedonian troops in three strategic locations: Corinth, Chalcis, and the Theban citadel of Cadmea.

An invasion of Persia must have seemed like a birthright to Alexander. After all, he had grown up with a father whose heart was set on it. In 334 BCE, Alexander the Great finally realized these long-held goals and initiated his military campaign by crossing the Hellespont, the site that marks the boundary between Europe and Asia. He left behind his faithful general, Antipater, as regent and a detachment of about thirteen thousand soldiers to defend Macedonian interests in Europe. Meanwhile, he traversed the Dardanelles with a combined Greek and Macedonian force of thirty-five thousand soldiers, including infantry, cavalry, archers, and javelin wielders.

Alexander's contemporary adversary, King Darius III of the Achaemenid Empire, has often been depicted in historical accounts as lacking courage and ineffective in his leadership. However, this is likely an unfair portrayal, as victors generally write history. What is more probable is that Alexander and his army outmatched Darius III. The first collision came at the Granicus River (present-day Biga), near the Sea of Marmara.

Facing Alexander and his Hellenic League were the Persian forces, commanded by Memnon of Rhodes and various other Persian *satraps*. The Persians had taken a defensive stance on the river's far bank, exploiting the steep and challenging embankment for protection. However, Alexander was renowned for his bold strategies. He initiated a daring maneuver by leading his elite Companion Cavalry in a charge directly across the Granicus River, engaging the Persians head-on. This unconventional approach caught the Persian forces off guard, as they had anticipated a more cautious strategy. Alexander broke their line despite the Persians' stubborn resistance, securing a decisive victory.

The consequences of this battle were profound. Alexander's triumph at Granicus solidified his status as a masterful military leader and substantially boosted his troops' morale. It also opened up the western regions of Asia Minor for further conquest, marking the inception of Alexander's campaign to liberate Greek cities from Persian rule. The Battle of Granicus set the stage for

Alexander's relentless march into the heart of the Persian Empire, shaping the course of history.

Immediately following the Persians' defeat at Granicus, most Greek cities in western Anatolia flung open their gates in welcome to Alexander's forces. After years of Persian occupation, most of these Anatolian *poleis* saw him as a liberator. This view was reinforced when he expelled the tyrants from these cities and set up democratic governments. Throughout the winter of 334 and 333 BCE, Alexander marched steadily eastward, bringing western Anatolia under his mantle.

While advancing through Asia Minor, Alexander paused in the city of Gordium in Phrygia, where he supposedly encountered the legendary Gordian Knot. According to the myth, an oracle had declared that whoever could unravel the intricate knot would become the ruler of Asia. Many attempted to untie it but failed due to the knot's intricate design. Faced with the challenge, Alexander approached the knot, and rather than trying to unravel it, he drew his sword and cut it in a decisive stroke.

Regardless of the story's authenticity, it symbolizes Alexander's problem-solving skills and showcases his unwavering determination and belief in his destined role as a conqueror. This act, along with his subsequent military successes, contributed to the legend of Alexander the Great as a charismatic and bold leader.

Persian and Greek forces met again at the Battle of Issus, a monumental clash in November 333 BCE. This decisive battle occurred near Issus in southern Anatolia near the modern-day town of Kinet Höyük. The battle was a Persian rout that devolved swiftly into chaos. Darius fled the battlefield, leaving his family and treasures behind. Alexander continued to march southward into Syria and Phoenicia. Darius offered peace terms twice: the second time included an exceedingly generous proposal to give Alexander ten thousand talents (a weight or unit of currency used by the Ancient Greeks and Romans) and to cede all Persian lands west of the Euphrates River to the young Macedonian for the return of his family. Alexander was not interested in ceasing his conquest, as evidenced by a supposed conversation with his second-in-command, Parmenio (or Parmenion), recorded by Plutarch. Upon seeing the terms offered by Darius III, Parmenio turned to Alexander and said, "I would accept, were I Alexander." Alexander quipped, "I would too, were I Parmenio."

The Greeks marched on, reaching Egypt by November of 332 BCE. He was largely welcomed here, and the Persian *satrap* Mazaces quietly surrendered. He was crowned at Memphis with the traditional double crown of the pharaohs and spent the remainder of the winter establishing administrative control over Egypt. In the spring of 331 BCE, with the entirety of the eastern Mediterranean coastline under his command, Alexander returned to Tyre in present-day Lebanon and prepared to advance his armies into Mesopotamia.

Darius and Alexander clashed again on the plains of Gaugamela near Nineveh (present-day Mosul in Iraq), and Darius retreated once again, moving eastward into Media. Alexander took Babylon and Susa and marched into Persia over the Zagros mountain range. Upon arrival in Persepolis, he burned the palace that had belonged to Xerxes I in revenge for the Greco-Persian Wars of the previous century.

Alexander did not intend to govern this vast new territory alone. He viewed it as a joint venture between Persia and Macedon, keeping many Persian *satraps* in positions of power. With Xerxes' palace burnt, Alexander viewed the Panhellenic revenge as fulfilled, allowing many of his Greek allies to return to their homeland.

Despite this dismissal of troops, Alexander was far from finished in Asia. In the summer of 330 BCE, Alexander marched east once more and learned that Darius III was dead. Killed near the modern-day town of Shāhrūd in Iran, Darius was stabbed by Bessus, the current *satrap* of Bactria. This region comprises parts of present-day Afghanistan, Tajikistan, and Uzbekistan. Alexander ordered Darius' body to be returned to Persepolis and buried with honors, but the revelation of his opponent's murder did not slacken his pace eastward.

With Darius now dead, Alexander could call himself the "Great King," and he set his sights on Bactria. Strategically vital, Bactria was a crossroads for trade and communication between what is typically considered the "East" and the "West." This region was under the rule of Bessus, the conniving *satrap* who had done away with Darius. Now declaring himself as the Great King and stirring up revolt in the eastern *satraps*, Bessus presented a problem for Alexander.

In 329 BCE, Bessus was apprehended by Alexander's general, Ptolemy. He was flogged, had his ears and nose cut off, and was finally executed at Ecbatana, near present-day Hamedan in Iran. With the threat of Bessus removed, Alexander's movement east quickened. Though challenged by rugged terrain, he was victorious over local populations and pockets of hostility his forces encountered.

In the same year as Bessus' capture and subsequent execution, Alexander arrived at the eastern boundary of the Persian empire, marked by the Jaxartes River, which is now known as the Syr Darya River, flowing through present-day Uzbekistan, Tajikistan, and Kazakhstan. There, he founded a city named Alexandria Eschate, which translates to "Alexandria the Farthest," and is located near the modern city of Khujand in northwestern Tajikistan.

By 327 BCE, Alexander was still facing resistance from the Bactrians, particularly a nobleman named Oxyartes and his followers. Oxyartes had served under Bessus and hid his wife and daughters in a supposedly impregnable fortress in Sogdiana—a site near the Zeravshan River in Uzbekistan. Unfortunately for Oxyartes, Alexander's forces breached the citadel and took his family captive. However, one of his daughters, Roxana (or Roxane), caught Alexander's eye. The pair were married, and Oxyartes hastily submitted to his new son-in-law.

In the summer of that same year, Alexander embarked on a campaign in India, taking his troops beyond the historic boundaries of the Persian Empire. After subduing Bactria, he now moved to cross the Hindu Kush mountains with a force estimated, by Plutarch, to be around one hundred and twenty thousand strong. This number is likely inflated, but it was still a credibly large contingent. He split his troops, sending half through the Khyber Pass to the south under the command of two cavalry leaders. He took the second half to the north, where he laid siege to Aornos, a sizeable natural stronghold near the Indus River that impeded his path into the Indian subcontinent. Ultimately, he could not pierce Aornos, but he successfully captured a hill across from the fortress and utilized his catapults to menace the Indians stationed there. They retreated but were killed by Alexander's men as they fled.

In June of 326 BCE, Alexander and his armies clashed with King Porus, the leader of a tribal kingdom in the

Punjab region of present-day Pakistan and India. Not much is known about Porus and his people; he is present in Western sources in conjunction with Alexander's story, but he is barely mentioned in contemporary Indian sources. Nevertheless, his territory was between the Hydaspes and Acesines rivers—known today as the Jhelum and Chenāb, respectively—and several of Porus' local rivals joined Alexander in his venture.

At the Hydaspes River, Alexander waged his final battle to conquer Asia. While his forces emerged victorious, he was deeply impressed by the bold tactics employed by Porus in leading his soldiers. Rather than deposing him, he allowed Porus to retain his crown and his lands, making him a vassal of Macedonia until his assassination at the hands of one of Alexander's generals, Eudemas, some years after Alexander's death.

After the Battle of Hydaspes, Alexander established two cities on the banks of the Hydaspes River: Alexandria Nicaea and Bucephala. The second was named to honor his faithful horse, Bucephalus, who perished in combat. After this, Alexander continued to press further eastward into India. Roughly two hundred miles from Porus' lands, Alexander and his army stopped on the banks of the Hyphasis (Beas) River. It is thought this is the farthest east that the young conqueror traveled, since there are no records of him reaching the Ganges or any other eastward landmarks.

On the banks of the Hyphasis, in the midst of pouring tropical rains, Alexander's weary troops dug their heels into the muddy ground. For the first time in the nearly eight years of campaigning, the majority of his army had lost the will to go on, even though their commander certainly intended to do so. According to the Greek historian Arrian of Nicomedia, his troops mutinied: "... the Macedonians had by now grown quite weary of their king's plans, seeing him charging from labor to labor, danger to danger." After three days of deliberation, Alexander decided to comply with his army's wishes, and leaving his easternmost territory in the hands of King Porus, he began to withdraw to the west.

The long march homeward was fraught, full of fighting, natural disasters, and a long, waterless march through the deserts of Gedrosia (Makran). Many became sick and died. By the spring of 324 BCE, Alexander had returned to Susa and realized that his vast empire was not well-organized or consolidated. Keen on unifying it, Alexander became attracted to the idea of mixing the various races he had conquered, despite this angering some of his Macedonian and Greek compatriots. While staying in the city, Alexander attempted to reconcile some of these issues by hosting a mass wedding for himself and eighty officers, all of whom took Persian wives. Alexander also gifted sizeable dowries to ten thousand soldiers who had taken Persian women for their spouses. Furthermore,

Alexander introduced soldiers of all nationalities into his army, including his elite Companion Cavalry.

This greatly upset the Macedonians, who saw Alexander's gradual interest in Asiatic traditions as threatening their positions of power and privilege. At the Babylonian city of Opis in 324 BCE, his troops mutinied in response to their king's continued push for integration. Over time, reconciliation was reached. However, Alexander began to display heightened signs of megalomania and emotional instability, increasingly embracing a belief in his own divinity.

In the spring of 323 BCE, Alexander welcomed delegations from various foreign nations in Babylon and started mapping out plans to explore the rivers and seas of his expansive empire. However, in June of that same year, Alexander mysteriously fell ill after a lively banquet and drinking session. Ten days later, on June 13, he was dead at only thirty-two or thirty-three years old. His massive empire was one of the largest in antiquity, and the blistering speed with which this territory was acquired remains truly remarkable. After all, Alexander the Great reigned for only twelve years.

The cause of his death is a subject of historical debate, with theories ranging from malaria and typhoid to strychnine poisoning. Mourned with divine honors in the Mediterranean world, his body was received in Alexandria, Egypt, by his former general, Ptolemy, and laid to rest in a coffin of gold. The young leader's final resting place was Alexandria, but his tomb was lost to the ages. General Ptolemy and Ptolemy I Soter refer to the same individual. He founded the influential Ptolemaic dynasty in Egypt, which remained in power until the Romans, led by Caesar Augustus (previously known as Octavian), annexed Egypt in 30 BCE.

Alexander's sudden and unexpected death left his empire in shambles as his generals (*Diadochi*) scrambled to gain control. Unity was impossible, and a series of power struggles, military conflicts, and shifting alliances ensued, ending with the *Diadochi* dividing the empire. He had passed without a clear successor, with his only legitimate child being his very young son, Alexander IV, by Roxana of Bactria.

Shortly after his death, Roxana had his second wife, the Persian woman he had married in Susa, executed before she left for Macedon. There, she rendezvoused with her late husband's mother, Olympias, and likely hoped to see her son take the Macedonian throne. It was not to be. Cassander, one of the *Diadochi*, proclaimed himself King of Macedonia and, in 316 BCE, captured Roxana and had her and her son executed.

The vast empire was not an empire for the ages but rather an empire bound to one man. With Alexander's death, unity vanished, and his *Diadochi* established their own empires within the realms of their former leader's accomplishments. These generals often fought one another, leading to the Wars of the Diadochi, or Successor Wars, that raged from 322 to 281 BCE. Ptolemy took Egypt, founding the Ptolemaic dynasty. Seleucus acquired vast territories, encompassing Asia Minor, Syria, Mesopotamia, and a significant portion of Persia. This led to the formation of the Seleucid Empire, which lasted until 64 BCE.

As for Greece and Macedonia, the region had been controlled by Alexander's longtime loyal general, Antipater, since the king had decamped to Asia. It remained under his control after Alexander's death, but as he neared the end himself, he proclaimed a man named Polyperchon the next ruler. This angered his son, Cassander, a general in his own right. He challenged Polyperchon's right to rule and found favor amongst the Greek city-states. He became the King of Macedonia in 316 BCE and ruled over most of Greece until he died in 297 BCE, marrying Alexander's half-sister, Thessalonike, to cement his legitimacy.

The death of Alexander the Great not only profoundly influenced ancient history but also left a significant and enduring legacy. His extensive conquests resulted in the establishment and continuation of Macedonian Greek rule across most of his empire long after his passing. This brought about the Hellenistic Era, during which Greek culture, art, and knowledge blended with other regions, leaving a lasting impact on the world. His early death ensured that the empire he built would be a short-lived but transformative force in the ancient world, influencing generations to come. Alexander's vision and ambition continue to captivate the imaginations of people around the globe, making him one of the most renowned figures in history.

The transition of Classical Greek culture into the Hellenistic world was slow. Hellenization did not happen all of a sudden with the death of Alexander in 323 BCE. It was a gradual process that had been underway since the first Greek colonizers set sail from their native islands and peninsulas.

The Ancient Greeks significantly influenced subsequent civilizations through their contributions to architecture, philosophy, governance, and religion. The following political superpower in the region, the Romans, took and adapted much of Ancient Greece, not least of which was their entire pantheon of deities. Greco-Roman thought directly fed the development of Europe, particularly during the Renaissance from 1450 to 1650 CE.

Greek influence spread to many major global powers, notably the British Empire, the most expansive empire in human history. Once a British colony, the United States of America has surpassed its former ruler in political influence and strength. Traces of Greek influence can still be observed in the foundations of American governance. Beyond Rome, Ancient Greece influenced the Byzantine

Empire, which in turn left a mark on the Slavic populations in its vicinity. Additionally, elements of Greek philosophy and thought are evident in the Islamic Golden Age that commenced in the 8th century CE.

As we close this journey through the history of Ancient Greece, I want to extend my heartfelt gratitude to you, the reader, for accompanying us on this captivating exploration. From humble beginnings as a cluster of modest villages amidst farmlands, Ancient Greece became an empire of unparalleled influence. Its artistic, cultural, philosophical, and political legacies have resonated through the ages, shaping continents from Asia to the Americas. In its story lies the essence of civilization's journey, a testament to the indomitable spirit of human endeavor. If this odyssey has enriched your understanding, I kindly ask that you consider leaving a review. Your insights not only guide others on their quest for knowledge but also help us enhance and refine our future endeavors. Together, we can ensure the legacy of Ancient Greece continues to inspire for many generations to come.

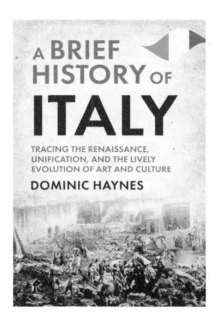

A Brief History of Italy: Tracing the Renaissance, Unification,
and the Lively Evolution of Art and Culture

A BRIEF
HISTORY OF
CENTRAL
BANKING

HOW THE QUEST FOR FINANCIAL STABILITY LED TO UNCONVENTIONAL MONETARY PRACTICES

DOMINIC HAYNES

A Brief History of Central Banking: How the Quest for Financial
Stability Led to Unconventional Monetary Practices

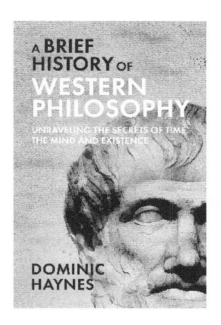

A Brief History of Western Philosophy: Unraveling the Secrets
of Time, the Mind, and Existence

REFERENCES

Becker, J. (2015, August 8). *Greek Architectural Orders.* Smart History.
https://smarthistory.org/greek-architectural-orders/

Britannica, T. Editors of Encyclopaedia (2018, March 12). *Abydos. Ency-*
clopedia

Britannica. https://www.britannica.com/place/Abydos-ancient-city-
Turkey

Britannica, T. Editors of Encyclopaedia (1998, July 20). *Alcmaeonid*
Family.

Encyclopedia Britannica. https://www.britannica.com/topic/Alcmaeonid-
family

Britannica, T. Editors of Encyclopaedia (2019, November 13). *Antipater.*
Encyclopedia

Britannica. https://www.britannica.com/biography/Antipater-regent-of-
Macedonia

Britannica, T. Editors of Encyclopaedia (1998, July 20). *apella. Ency-*
clopedia

Britannica. https://www.britannica.com/topic/apella

Britannica, T. Editors of Encyclopaedia (2016, December 15). *Aristagoras.*
Encyclopedia Britannica. https://www.britannica.com/biography/
Aristagoras

Britannica, T. Editors of Encyclopaedia (2016, December 15). *Aris-*
tomenes.

Encyclopedia Britannica. https://www.britannica.com/biography/Aris
tomenes

Britannica, T. Editors of Encyclopaedia (2016, December 13). *Artabanus.*
Encyclopedia

Britannica. https://www.britannica.com/biography/Artabanus

Britannica, T. Editors of Encyclopaedia (2020, April 3). *Battle of Issus.*
Encyclopedia

Britannica. https://www.britannica.com/event/Battle-of-Issus-Persian-
history

Britannica, T. Editors of Encyclopaedia (2023, September 15). *Battle of Marathon.*
Encyclopedia Britannica. https://www.britannica.com/event/Battle-of-Marathon

Britannica, T. Editors of Encyclopaedia (2023, September 15). *Battle of Salamis.*
Encyclopedia Britannica. https://www.britannica.com/event/Battle-of-Salamis

Britannica, T. Editors of Encyclopaedia (2020, May 17). *Bessus. Encyclopedia*
Britannica. https://www.britannica.com/biography/Bessus

Britannica, T. Editors of Encyclopaedia (2018, August 15). *Boeotia. Encyclopedia*
Britannica. https://www.britannica.com/place/Boeotia

Britannica, T. Editors of Encyclopaedia (1998, July 20). *Boeotian League.*
Encyclopedia
Britannica. https://www.britannica.com/topic/Boeotian-League

Britannica, T. Editors of Encyclopaedia (2023, April 14). *Cadmus. Encyclopedia*
Britannica. https://www.britannica.com/topic/Cadmus

Britannica, T. Editors of Encyclopaedia (2020, April 3). *Cambyses II.*
Encyclopedia
Britannica. https://www.britannica.com/biography/Cambyses-II

Britannica, T. Editors of Encyclopaedia (2007, October 19). *Carneia.*
Encyclopedia
Britannica. https://www.britannica.com/topic/Carneia

Britannica, T. Editors of Encyclopaedia (2015, April 1). *Conon. Encyclopedia*
Britannica. https://www.britannica.com/biography/Conon-Greek-admiral

Britannica, T. Editors of Encyclopaedia (2009, April 27). *Council of the Four Hundred.*
Encyclopedia Britannica. https://www.britannica.com/topic/Council-of-the-Four-Hundred

Britannica, T. Editors of Encyclopaedia (2021, December 21). *Cyclades.*
Encyclopedia

Britannica. https://www.britannica.com/place/Cyclades

Britannica, T. Editors of Encyclopaedia (2014, April 15). *Cyrene. Encyclopedia Britannica.* https://www.britannica.com/place/Cyrene-ancient-Greek-colony-Libya

Britannica, T. Editors of Encyclopaedia (2007, October 18). *Cyzicus. Encyclopedia Britannica.* https://www.britannica.com/place/Cyzicus-ancient-Turkey

Britannica, T. Editors of Encyclopaedia (2023, February 26). *Darius III. Encyclopedia Britannica.* https://www.britannica.com/biography/Darius-III

Britannica, T. Editors of Encyclopaedia (2020, April 3). *Delian League. Encyclopedia Britannica.* https://www.britannica.com/topic/Delian-League

Britannica, T. Editors of Encyclopaedia (2017, December 19). *Dorian. Encyclopedia Britannica.* https://www.britannica.com/topic/Dorian

Britannica, T. Editors of Encyclopaedia (2018, April 2). *Ecclesia. Encyclopedia Britannica.* https://www.britannica.com/topic/Ecclesia-ancient-Greek-assembly

Britannica, T. Editors of Encyclopaedia (1998, July 20). *eupatrid. Encyclopedia Britannica.* https://www.britannica.com/topic/eupatrid

Britannica, T. Editors of Encyclopaedia and Riley, P. (2022, February 7). *Events of the Ancient Olympic Games. Encyclopedia Britannica.* https://www.britannica.com/story/ancient-olympic-games

Britannica, T. Editors of Encyclopaedia (2023, August 22). *Greco-Persian Wars. Encyclopedia Britannica.* https://www.britannica.com/event/Greco-Persian-Wars

Britannica, T. Editors of Encyclopaedia (2020, April 3). *Hecataeus of Miletus. Encyclopedia Britannica.* https://www.britannica.com/biography/Hecataeus-of-Miletus

Britannica, T. Editors of Encyclopaedia (2016, October 7). *Hellen. Encyclopedia Britannica.* https://www.britannica.com/topic/Hellen

Britannica, T. Editors of Encyclopaedia (2019, November 5). *helot. Encyclopedia Britannica.* https://www.britannica.com/money/topic/helot

Britannica, T. Editors of Encyclopaedia (2023, August 3). *Hippias. Encyclopedia Britannica.* https://www.britannica.com/biography/Hippias

Britannica, T. Editors of Encyclopaedia (2016, December 15). *Histiaeus. Encyclopedia Britannica.* https://www.britannica.com/biography/Histiaeus

Britannica, T. Editors of Encyclopaedia (2017, December 19). *Ionian. Encyclopedia Britannica.* https://www.britannica.com/topic/Ionian

Britannica, T. Editors of Encyclopaedia (2012, March 6). *Isthmian Games. Encyclopedia Britannica.* https://www.britannica.com/sports/Isthmian-Games

Britannica, T. Editors of Encyclopaedia (2016, March 14). *Khujand. Encyclopedia Britannica.* https://www.britannica.com/place/Khujand

Britannica, T. Editors of Encyclopaedia (2017, December 19). *Lelantine War. Encyclopedia Britannica.* https://www.britannica.com/event/Lelantine-War

Britannica, T. Editors of Encyclopaedia (2023, February 12). *Leonidas. Encyclopedia Britannica.* https://www.britannica.com/biography/Leonidas-king-of-Sparta

Britannica, T. Editors of Encyclopaedia (2018, August 9). *Leucas. Encyclopedia Britannica.* https://www.britannica.com/place/Leucas-island-Greece

Britannica, T. Editors of Encyclopaedia (2021, May 13). *Lycurgus. Encyclopedia Britannica.* https://www.britannica.com/topic/Lycurgus-Spartan-lawgiver

Britannica, T. Editors of Encyclopaedia (2020, April 3). *Mardonius. Encyclopedia Britannica.* https://www.britannica.com/biography/Mardonius

Britannica, T. Editors of Encyclopaedia (2020, April 3). *Media. Encyclopedia Britannica.* https://www.britannica.com/place/Media-ancient-region-Iran

Britannica, T. Editors of Encyclopaedia (2018, August 9). *Megara. Encyclopedia Britannica.* https://www.britannica.com/place/Megara-Greece

Britannica, T. Editors of Encyclopaedia (2019, November 13). *Menderes River. Encyclopedia Britannica.* https://www.britannica.com/place/Menderes-River

Britannica, T. Editors of Encyclopaedia (2016, April 1). *Messenian Wars. Encyclopedia Britannica.* https://www.britannica.com/event/Messenian-Wars

Britannica, T. Editors of Encyclopaedia (2023, August 21). *Miletus. Encyclopedia Britannica.* https://www.britannica.com/place/Miletus

Britannica, T. Editors of Encyclopaedia (2023, August 28). *Minoan civilization. Encyclopedia Britannica.* https://www.britannica.com/topic/Minoan-civilization

Britannica, T. Editors of Encyclopaedia (2007, December 17). *Naukratis. Encyclopedia Britannica.* https://www.britannica.com/place/Naukratis

Britannica, T. Editors of Encyclopaedia (2010, September 26). *Nemean Games. Encyclopedia Britannica.* https://www.britannica.com/sports/Nemean-Games

Britannica, T. Editors of Encyclopaedia (2019, November 6). *Opis. Encyclopedia Britannica.* https://www.britannica.com/place/Opis

Britannica, T. Editors of Encyclopaedia (2020, February 6). *Pausanias. Encyclopedia*

Britannica. https://www.britannica.com/biography/Pausanias-Greek-military-officer

Britannica, T. Editors of Encyclopaedia (2019, November 5). *Peloponnesian League.*

Encyclopedia Britannica. https://www.britannica.com/topic/Peloponnesian-League

Britannica, T. Editors of Encyclopaedia (2023, August 29). *Peloponnesian War.*

Encyclopedia Britannica. https://www.britannica.com/event/Peloponnesian-War

Britannica, T. Editors of Encyclopaedia (2013, October 11). *Pindus Mountains.*

Encyclopedia Britannica. https://www.britannica.com/place/Pindus-Mountains

Britannica, T. Editors of Encyclopaedia (2020, April 3). *Porus. Encyclopedia*

Britannica. https://www.britannica.com/biography/Porus

Britannica, T. Editors of Encyclopaedia (2008, April 28). *Pythian Games. Encyclopedia*

Britannica. https://www.britannica.com/sports/Pythian-Games

Britannica, T. Editors of Encyclopaedia (2023, September 22). *Roxana. Encyclopedia*

Britannica. https://www.britannica.com/biography/Roxana

Britannica, T. Editors of Encyclopaedia (2019, November 12). *Siege of Aornos.*

Encyclopedia Britannica. https://www.britannica.com/event/Siege-of-Aornos

Britannica, T. Editors of Encyclopaedia (2020, March 31). *Solon's laws. Encyclopedia*

Britannica. https://www.britannica.com/topic/Solons-laws

Britannica, T. Editors of Encyclopaedia (2014, May 9). *Sybaris. Encyclopedia*

Britannica. https://www.britannica.com/place/Sybaris

Britannica, T. Editors of Encyclopaedia (2023, October 13). *Temple of Artemis.*

Encyclopedia Britannica. https://www.britannica.com/topic/Temple-of-Artemis-temple-Ephesus-Turkey

Britannica, T. Editors of Encyclopaedia (2023, July 14). *Thebes. Encyclopedia Britannica.* https://www.britannica.com/place/Thebes-Greece

Burckhardt, J. (1999). *The Greeks and Greek Civilization.* St. Martin's Griffin.

Cadoux, T. (2022, October 7). *Solon. Encyclopedia Britannica.* https://www.britannica.com/biography/Solon

Carney, J. (2013, September 13). *The Ancient and Noble Greek Tradition of Debt Repudiation.* CNBC. https://www.cnbc.com/2011/06/03/the-ancient-and-noble-greek-tradition-of-debt-repudiation.html

Cartwright, M. (2016, April 8). *Cleisthenes.* World History Encyclopedia. https://www.worldhistory.org/Cleisthenes/

Cartwright, M. (2013, June 5). *Corcyra.* World History Encyclopedia. https://www.worldhistory.org/corcyra/

Cartwright, M. (2009, September 2). *Corinth.* World History Encyclopedia. https://www.worldhistory.org/corinth/

Cartwright, M. (2012, October 23). *Cyclades.* World History Encyclopedia. https://www.worldhistory.org/Cyclades/

Cartwright, M. (2018, March 29). *Minoan Civilization.* World History Encyclopedia. https://www.worldhistory.org/Minoan_Civilization/

Cartwright, M. (2019, October 2). *Mycenaean Civilization.* World History Encyclopedia. https://www.worldhistory.org/Mycenaean_Civilization/

Cartwright, M. (2016, March 9). *Peloponnesian League.* World History Encyclopedia. https://www.worldhistory.org/Peloponnesian_League/

Cartwright, M. (2018, May 2). *Peloponnesian War.* World History Encyclopedia. https://www.worldhistory.org/Peloponnesian_War/

Cartwright, M. (2016, March 10). *Solon.* World History Encyclopedia.

https://www.worldhistory.org/solon/

Cartwright, M. (2018, July 24). *Statue of Zeus at Olympia.* World History Encyclopedia. https://www.worldhistory.org/Statue_of_Zeus_at_Olympia/

Coleman, J. (2000). An Archaeological Scenario for the "Coming of the Greeks" ca.

3200 B.C. *The Journal of Indo-European Studies* 28(1–2): 101–154. https://www.academia.edu/4908240

Cyzicus. (2021, December 21). Turkish Archaeological News. https://turkisharchaeonews.net/site/cyzicus

Diestch, D. and Stern, R. (2021, November 11). *Greek Architecture: Doric, Ionic, or*

Corinthian?. Architecture for Dummies. https://www.dummies.com/article/academics-the-arts/art-architecture/architecture/greek-architecture-doric-ionic-or-corinthian-201218/

Dunn, D. (2020, January 9). *Did the Trojan War actually happen?.* BBC. https://www.bbc.com/culture/article/20200106-did-the-trojan-war-actually-happen

Frye, R. N. (2023, August 18). *Cyrus the Great. Encyclopedia Britannica.* https://www.britannica.com/biography/Cyrus-the-Great

Gill, N. (2018, August 25). *The Great Ionian Colony of Miletus.* ThoughtCo. https://www.thoughtco.com/miletus-greek-history-119714

Gill, N. (2020, January 28). *King Porus of Paurava.* ThoughtCo. https://www.thoughtco.com/king-porus-of-paurava-116851

Grant, R. (2020, June). *The King and the Conqueror.* Smithsonian Magazine. https://www.smithsonianmag.com/history/philip-macedonia-even-greater-alexander-the-great-180974878/

Griffith, G. Thompson (2023, August 22). *Philip II. Encyclopedia Britannica.* https://www.britannica.com/biography/Philip-II-king-of-Macedonia

Havarti, K., Röding, C., Bosman, A.M., et al. (2019, July 25). Apidima cave fossils

provide earliest evidence of Homo sapiens in Eurasia. Nature 571: 500–504. https://doi.org/10.1038/s41586-019-1376-z

Hayward, L. (2020, May 27). *The 6 Most Important Greek Gods You Should Know*. The Collector. https://www.thecollector.com/greek-gods/

History.com Editors. (2023, June 5). *Ancient Greek Democracy*. History.com. https://www.history.com/topics/ancient-greece/ancient-greece-democracy

History.com Editors. (2023, June 22). *Peloponnesian War*. History.com. https://www.history.com/topics/ancient-greece/peloponnesian-war

History.com Editors. (2023, June 23). *The Olympic Games*. History.com. https://www.history.com/topics/sports/olympic-games

Hornblower, S. (2023, September 4). *Ancient Greek civilization*. Encyclopedia Britannica. https://www.britannica.com/place/ancient-Greece

Huot, J. (2023, September 8). *Xerxes I*. Encyclopedia Britannica. https://www.britannica.com/biography/Xerxes-I

Katz, B. (2019, July 11). *This 210,000-Year-Old Skull May Be The Oldest Human Fossil Found in Europe*. Smithsonian Magazine. https://www.smithsonianmag.com/smart-news/210000-skull-may-be-oldest-human-fossil-found-europe-180972629/

Kiersted, J. (2017, August 27). *The uncertain origins of the modern marathon*. The Conversation. https://theconversation.com/the-uncertain-origins-of-the-modern-marathon-79493

Lewis, D. (2023, September 22). *Pericles*. Encyclopedia Britannica. https://www.britannica.com/biography/Pericles-Athenian-statesman

Lewis, S. (2023, October 3). *tyranny*. Encyclopedia Britannica. https://www.britannica.com/topic/tyranny

Lucian. (2023). A Slip of the Tongue In Greeting - The Works of Lucian. Loeb Classical Library. DOI: 10.4159/DLCL.lucian-slip_tongue_greeting.1959

Mark J. (2022, February 16). *Aristarchus of Samos*. World History Encyclopedia. https://www.worldhistory.org/Aristarchus_of_Samos/

Mark, J. (2023, July 27). *Greek Dark Age*. World History Encyclopedia.

https://www.worldhistory.org/Greek_Dark_Age/

Mark, J. (2021, June 17). *Sacred Band of Thebes*. World History Encyclopedia.
https://www.worldhistory.org/Sacred_Band_of_Thebes/

Mark, J. (2019, October 22). *Seleucid Empire*. World History Encyclopedia.
https://www.worldhistory.org/Seleucid_Empire/

Mark, J. (2021, June 14). *Spartan Women*. World History Encyclopedia.
https://www.worldhistory.org/article/123/spartan-women/

Matthew, P. (2020, November 6). *The Hyphasis Mutiny*. World History Encyclopedia.
https://www.worldhistory.org/article/1630/the-hyphasis-mutiny/

Matthews, R. (2017, March 24). *Battle of Granicus*. Encyclopedia Britannica.
https://www.britannica.com/event/Battle-of-the-Granicus-334BCE

Matthews, R. (2017, March 23). *Battle of the Hydaspes*. Encyclopedia Britannica.
https://www.britannica.com/event/Battle-of-the-Hydaspes

Meiggs, R. (2023, March 10). *Cleisthenes of Athens*. Encyclopedia Britannica.
https://www.britannica.com/biography/Cleisthenes-of-Athens

Miate, L. (2023, June 13). *Pelops*. World History Encyclopedia.
https://www.worldhistory.org/Pelops/

Mingren, W. (2022, February 25). *Olbia: Greek, Scythian, Roman Trading Center That Had Dolphin Money*. Ancient Origins. https://www.ancient-origins.net/history-ancient-traditions/olbia-0016462

Mishra, S., Mengestab, A., and Khosa, S. (2022, April 14). Historical Perspectives and Medical Maladies of Alexander the Great. Cureus 14(4). 10.7759/cureus.23925

Mistriotis, A. (2014, March 20). *The Greek Strategy at the Battle of Salamis, 480 BCE*. World History Encyclopedia. https://www.worldhistory.org/article/671/the-greek-strategy-at-the-battle-of-salamis-480-bc/

Miszczac, I. (2023, June 24). *Miletus*. Turkish Archaeological News. https://turisharchaeonews.net/site/miletus

Munn-Rankin, J. (2023, March 3). *Darius I. Encyclopedia Britannica.*

https://www.britannica.com/biography/Darius-I

Olympic History: From the Home of Zeus in Olympia to the Modern Games.
(n.d.).

International Olympic Committee. https://olympics.com/ioc/ancient-olympic-games/history

Plutarch. (1962). *Moralia.* Harvard University Press.

Smith, W. (1873). *A Dictionary of Greek and Roman Biography and Mythology.*
Spottiswoode and Co.

Starr, C. G. (2019, April 4). *Peisistratus. Encyclopedia Britannica.*
https://www.britannica.com/biography/Peisistratus

Stillwell, R., MacDonald, W., McAllister, M., et al. (1976). *MASSALIA or Massilia*
(Marseille) Bouches-du-Rhône, France. The Princeton Encyclopedia of Classical Sites. https://www.perseus.tufts.edu/hopper/text?doc=Perseus:text:1999.04.0006:entry=massalia

Tourloukis, V. and Havarti, K. (2017, April 24). The Palaeolithic record of Greece: A
synthesis of the evidence and a research agenda for the future. Quaternary International 466:1–18. DOI:10.1016/j.quaint.2017.04.020

Tuma, E. H. (2022, December 9). *land reform. Encyclopedia Britannica.*
https://www.britannica.com/money/topic/land-reform

Walbank, F. W. (2023, October 5). *Alexander the Great. Encyclopedia Britannica.*
https://www.britannica.com/biography/Alexander-the-Great

Waldmann, N. (2019, January 14). *The Ancient Greek Kouros and Kore.* Daily Art
Magazine. https://www.dailyartmagazine.com/ancient-greek-kouros-and-kore/

Wasson, D. (2013, February 21). *Byzantium.* World History Encyclopedia.
https://www.worldhistory.org/Byzantium/

Wasson, D. (2016, June 23). *Cassander.* World History Encyclopedia.
https://www.worldhistory.org/Cassander/

Wasson, D. (2013, June 1). *Olympias.* World History Encyclopedia.
https://www.worldhistory.org/Olympias/

Wasson, D. (2022, November 28). *Tyrants of Greece*. World History Encyclopedia.
https://www.worldhistory.org/article/2117/tyrants-of-greece/

Welcome to the Ancient Olympic Games. (n.d.). International Olympic Committee.
https://olympics.com/ioc/ancient-olympic-games

Werner, R. (2023, October 12). *Ptolemy I Soter*. *Encyclopedia Britannica*.
https://www.britannica.com/biography/Ptolemy-I-Soter

Made in the USA
Las Vegas, NV
21 September 2024

95554889R00094